"As a tradfi expert who took an early deep-dive into the crazy world of cryptocurrencies, Hoe Lon provides a unique perspective. In 'Deflated', he unpacks and demystifies the rapid developments and innovations in the digital asset space. And he does so with a deeply personal touch.

It is easy to get swept up in the frenzy, excess and volatility in crypto. This book is an effort to reflect and understand by someone who is truly passionate about the space and it's values. I invite you to take a glimpse into what I've experienced first-hand from working with Hoe Lon these past few years."

—**Darius Sit**
Co-Founder of QCP Capital and Philip Street Partners.

Hoe Lon's latest book is excellent and I strongly recommend it to anyone interested in crypto, capital markets, trading, or human resilience. The book is really two books in one. First, you get an expert look at blockchain investing that will keep you sane through the cyclical ups and downs. Second, you get a series of Market Wizards style interviews with some of the best in the trading business. Tons of great information and inspiration in a tight, well-written package.

—**Brent Donnelly**
President of Spectra Markets.

DEFLATED

DEFLATED

How to Find Your Footing in a Shaky Blockchain Investment World

Leng Hoe Lon

© 2021 Leng Hoe Lon & Marshall Cavendish International (Asia) Private Limited

Published by Marshall Cavendish Business
An imprint of Marshall Cavendish International

All rights reserved

No part of this publication may be reproduced, stored in a retrieval system or transmitted, in any form or by any means, electronic, mechanical, photocopying, recording or otherwise, without the prior permission of the copyright owner. Requests for permission should be addressed to the Publisher, Marshall Cavendish International (Asia) Private Limited, 1 New Industrial Road, Singapore 536196. Tel: (65) 6213 9300. E-mail: genref@sg.marshallcavendish.com
Website: www.marshallcavendish.com

The publisher makes no representation or warranties with respect to the contents of this book, and specifically disclaims any implied warranties or merchantability or fitness for any particular purpose, and shall in no event be liable for any loss of profit or any other commercial damage, including but not limited to special, incidental, consequential, or other damages.

Other Marshall Cavendish Offices:
Marshall Cavendish Corporation, 800 Westchester Ave, Suite N-641, Rye Brook, NY 10573, USA • Marshall Cavendish International (Thailand) Co Ltd, 253 Asoke, 16th Floor, Sukhumvit 21 Road, Klongtoey Nua, Wattana, Bangkok 10110, Thailand • Marshall Cavendish (Malaysia) Sdn Bhd, Times Subang, Lot 46, Subang Hi-Tech Industrial Park, Batu Tiga, 40000 Shah Alam, Selangor Darul Ehsan, Malaysia

Marshall Cavendish is a registered trademark of Times Publishing Limited

National Library Board, Singapore Cataloguing-in-Publication Data

Name(s): Leng, Hoe Lon.
Title: Deflated : how to find your footing in a shaky blockchain investment world / Leng Hoe Lon.
Description: Singapore : Marshall Cavendish Business, [2021]
Identifier(s): ISBN 978-981-5009-32-3 (paperback)
Subject(s): LCSH: Cryptocurrencies. | Blockchains (Databases) | Investments.
Classification: DDC 332.4—dc23

Printed in Singapore

Cover art by Aaron Gan

Disclaimer
This publication is for information purposes only, and does not constitute investment or financial advice.

To all the traders in the world.
The machines have now eaten our lunch,
They still have not learned our gut instincts,
Don't stop believing,
We are resilient.

To all the people in the world.
We suffered, we fell, but we are no victims,
Embrace negatives, tune in the positives,
Don't stop living,
We are resilient.

To all the children in the world.
Challenges are part of life, and it is not only you,
Thrive in adversity, follow through with your goals,
Don't stop dreaming,
We are resilient.

This book is dedicated to you, the reader – for choosing
to accept the good, hope and strength.

CONTENTS

Foreword		9
Introduction: When Good Products Turn Bad		15

Part I: A Maturing Market

Chapter 1	Bubble Trouble	28
Chapter 2	These Turbulent Coins: Why Crypto is Here to Stay	47
Chapter 3	The Emerging New Market	61
Chapter 4	From Currency to Token	76
Chapter 5	Emerging from Crypto Winter	94

Part II: Visions from the Trenches

Chapter 6	Getting Your Rhythm Back: An Interview with Paul Tudor Jones	106
Chapter 7	Manufacturing Luck: An Interview with Vishal Agrawal	118
Chapter 8	The Future of Decentralised Finance: An Interview with Loi Luu	133
Chapter 9	Conquering Fear and Stepping Up: An Interview with Jimmy Lim	145

Conclusion: Bouncing Back Higher	159
Glossary	167
Appendix: Day One Advice for New Hedge Fund Managers	178
Acknowledgements	187
About the Author	188
About the Co-Author and the Cover Artist	189
Fundraising for Futuremakers	190

FOREWORD

I am an orchestra conductor and, to put it simply, I wave a little white stick in front of orchestras and perform in different concert halls and theatres around the world. I started my journey as a professional conductor in 2016 and by 2019, I was established as a specialist in opera and ballet in Russia.

I had my sights set on Europe and the rest of the world, winning some accolades along the way. I was an assistant conductor to the prominent French conductor Yan Pascal Tortelier with the Iceland Symphony Orchestra and the BBC Philharmonic, and the first foreign, Asian and Singaporean assistant conductor of the Perm Opera and Ballet Theatre, near Russia's Ural Mountains, which ranks just behind the famous Mariinsky and Bolshoi Theatres in Russia, and to open the Linkhovoin Opera Festival in Russia on its 80th anniversary.

I was also the permanent guest conductor of the Mariinsky Theatre's North Ossetia-Alania branch (a well-known theatre in south-western Russia, just across the border from Georgia), and a protégé of the legendary Italian conductor Riccardo Muti at the Spring Festival in Tokyo. It would never have occurred to me that anything would stop me from conducting.

My name is Amos Chiya and at the time of writing, I'm back home in Singapore and working for Deliveroo.

So, the pandemic happened. Concert halls and theatres were closed. Travel restrictions were imposed. Thousands of us artists from all sectors of the performing arts became fearful for our future. I was 30 years old, unemployed and in Russia, a foreign land. I searched for work while taking what music-related jobs I could, including teaching piano privately.

It didn't work, and my savings ran out after just under a year. With less than $20 in my bank account, I was forced to return home to Singapore. I was back in December 2020, and despite applying for more than 40 jobs, including sales, management and academic positions, I received rejections from every single one of them.

Facing financial instability, I found myself feeling depressed and anxious. I was constantly feeling frustrated and dejected. Wanting to do something useful, I applied to be a food delivery rider and started working ten to 12-hour shifts, six days a week.

Not only did the job get me back on my feet, it gave me different perspectives and insights while encountering people in different situations and from all walks of life. It's given me a lot more courage, strength and happiness, and also made me feel calmer and more contented. I know that I have continued to bring a little joy to people's lives, just as I used to do through music.

Four months later, I've also found myself to have grown more introspective and mindful, with a clearer sense of purpose. This book brought home the lessons I learned in those months delivering food under the hot sun, such as the need to be realistic and how to manage through uncertainty.

Veteran trader and blockchain advisor Leng Hoe Lon saw my story in the news, and reached out through Instagram. He invited me to meet his friends from work and his personal life. That sharing gave me energy and guidance, and motivated me to keep pursuing my dreams in the world of music.

Personally, he is an intellect, a visionary ... and a great cook. I was extremely flattered when he asked me to write this foreword, and I immediately agreed! Indeed, I have been "Deflated", but am now on track to start conducting again in Tokyo. If you ever feel down, please know that you are never alone by yourself!

Life is full of ups and downs, but the last few years seem to have given us far more downs than usual. On top of the volatile nature of cryptocurrencies, we've seen many of the most promising new blockchain developments run aground, go on hiatus or collapse altogether. The freer, more decentralised future we once spoke of seems even further away, as promises come under the cold light of reality.

But in the same way a savvy investor looks at the longer time frame, Hoe Lon shows that the world of cryptocurrencies, blockchain tokens and their derivatives isn't disappearing. It's evolving into an entirely new ecosystem of interconnected, decentralised and self-running applications, yet overseen by a new, informed network of checks and balances. As a result, these survivors are now more valuable, in demand and useful than ever.

This book is your primer to blockchain's potential in the 2020s and beyond. In this follow-up to *Decrypted*, his tell-all guide to cryptocurrencies and blockchain, Hoe Lon takes you into the exciting new frontier of blockchain use, and gives much-needed advice from the best investors the field has to offer. You'll learn how to focus your investments, recover from any bad trades that might have emerged from the difficult "crypto winter" years of the late 2010s and set yourself up to reap the growth of a brighter, better future for all of us.

Amos Chiya

INTRODUCTION: WHEN GOOD PRODUCTS TURN BAD

> Son, your ego is writing cheques your body can't cash.
> **Captain Jordan, *Top Gun* (1986)**

What You'll Learn
- The cycle of technological booms and busts, and why cryptocurrencies and blockchain are no exceptions.
- The need to be realistic about what it can and cannot do, and how failure to do this has led to unwarranted hype.
- How the hype brought the market crashing down, and how we can manage uncertainty.

On a recent flight to Jakarta, a documentary on the rise of the Internet over the past 50 years caught my eye. Half a century ago, the Internet was coming into existence as a means for computers to "talk" to each other around the world. At each new phase of its growth, various companies were established to provide services around each new development – for instance, basic connection service in the 1970s, email in the 1980s, online shopping in the 1990s and software distribution in the 2000s. Every online service we use and take for granted today has been the winner of a fierce, literal winner-take-all battle for dominance.

This is a very rough generalisation, but if history has been any guide, it's told us that while dozens of companies may start in a dot-com boom, very few will still be around when the dust settles. These would be the firms that have read the trends of the future correctly, and will be in a position to take advantage of them.

And these are the firms whose shares reward their investors handsomely. As my friend Adam Levinson, Managing Partner and CIO of venture firm Graticule Asset Management Asia, reminded us in his Introduction to my book, *Decrypted*: "The price of any new commodity usually rises and falls in waves, as the world comes to terms with it."

Perhaps cryptocurrencies are undergoing the same boom-and-bust process on their road to mass adoption, just at an accelerated pace. Out of the gate, Bitcoin shot up in value, but like the turbulence you feel in an aeroplane cabin, it crashed down just as quickly. A number of merchants started accepting bitcoins as payment, only to stop when the tokens' volatility meant prices couldn't stay constant. A high-profile example is Valve Software's gaming distribution service Steam, which began taking Bitcoin payments in April 2017, only to stop in December, citing "high fees and volatility".

As it took time for bitcoins to be transferred successfully, they could change dramatically in value during the transfer interval. If there was a shortfall, customers would have to add more bitcoins ... and more and more were getting "caught out a second time as the value changed again".[1]

BBC Technology further noted ominously: "Valve's decision comes as crypto-cash mining market NiceHash reported a 'security breach' had meant hackers had accessed its Bitcoin wallet, which had contained about $60m in bitcoins." It was reported in August 2018 that most of the stolen money had been returned, although NiceHash founder Matjaz Skorjanc faced charges of malware creation and distribution.[2]

Burger King, which had some European branches beginning to accept bitcoins and even launched its own Whoppercoin crypto, eventually stopped doing so at the end of May 2019, just three years after this experiment began in 2016.[3]

Imagine making enough to enjoy a tidy profit today, then having the same amount not even cover the rent tomorrow! Before it can go mainstream as a medium of exchange, users and recipients must first believe in it, in the same way they believe that governments will honour the value printed on banknotes. It appears that Bitcoin's use as a value store, however inconsistent its value might be, has won out over its use as a medium of exchange. The latter is only likely to take place if traditional means of payment and value exchange are absent or unreliable. Bitcoin developer and writer Jimmy Song sums it up well:[4]

> Lots of options exist for method of payment, but very few for store of value and none that are as confiscation-resistant as Bitcoin is.
>
> As Bitcoin adoption grows, merchants will start demanding Bitcoin *as a store of value* in lieu of any

> other currency. This is already happening to a degree in places like Turkey, Iran and Venezuela. When a large part of society wants Bitcoin as a store of value, only then will the method of payment use case emerge en masse.

Other blockchain-based companies haven't been able to turn the promises they made into reality; they may have raised large amounts of money, but did not know what to do with it. Perhaps founders leave, they pivot to something else, or simply disappear with the money they've raised.

"Cryptocurrency might one day disrupt finance, online betting, gaming, logistics, and content creation, among other industries, but none of that has happened yet," notes Stan Schroeder at *Mashable*.[5] Research advisory firm Gartner calls this a "hype cycle" in which "blockchain is sliding into the Trough of Disillusionment", where "interest has waned as experiments and implementations fail to deliver."[6]

To paraphrase the line in the movie *Top Gun*, companies are writing cheques that the technology can't cash yet. While some of this can be excused as the opening throes of a new market, it does speak to the tendency to make grand promises that may not pan out, and the need for government regulation, not to prevent this so much as to help investors ensure they aren't throwing good money after bad. This process may sound Darwinian (and in many ways it is) but it helps to weed out scams or bad ideas at the start.

But there's reason for hope. Crypto is maturing, not going away, and with powerful new players like Facebook's own Diem coin, the possibilities are just as endless today as they were when Satoshi Nakamoto revealed Bitcoin to the world. The idea is to manage your expectations and invest wisely, because no matter what happens, the fundamentals aren't going to change. The market is simply growing bigger, and as cybersecurity giants Kaspersky noted in their 2019 cryptocurrency report:[7]

> The idea of using cryptocurrency is resonating with consumers, and following the global rise of digital and biometric payments, many analysts and financial industry experts predict cryptocurrency to follow suit. The onboarding of new users and cryptocurrency adoption continues to rise. In fact, the number of verified cryptocurrency users has almost doubled in the past year.
>
> ...
>
> Part of the problem could be down to how new and unproven the technology is. With many of us happy to manage our finances and investments with tried and tested methods, such as traditional bank accounts or stocks and shares, we clearly seek credibility when handling our finances.

In *Decrypted*, I talked about the rise of cryptocurrencies as a powerful new financial product, and shared my thoughts on the issues surrounding their value and use, as well as the underlying technology, known as blockchain. The financial world has changed a lot in the decade since Bitcoin was introduced, but that change has not been smooth sailing. There are literally thousands of cryptocurrencies today, but Bitcoin remains the standard by which they are measured.

The ups and downs of cryptocurrency prices are still waves to be ridden, and I want to share the best surfing tips I have to help you make sure you're making the best possible decisions before you're pulled under – and if that happens, how to regain your balance and seek out the next big wave. Don't worry if you've been burned; I'll show you how the crypto market is likely to change and how you can recover from your losses.

In this book, I will take you through the reality check I feel the financial market has undergone. When mainstream wealth assets like fiat (that is, government-issued currencies like the Singapore dollar), stocks, shares and bonds are affected, cryptos tend to follow suit. In this regard, they function like any other financial product. I'll also share my thoughts on what to do so that your crypto wealth is as secure as you can make it. As for blockchain, it now appears to be a solution in search of a problem, but the technology is still so new that exactly what problems it can tackle will be as much of a focus as ever.

It's been up and down; I'm not exaggerating when I say the process has been adrenaline-pumping. Even today, it excites me to see how the community has soldiered on. Crypto arrived on the futures exchange to lots of fanfare, but people soon realised that the solutions it promised were still a long way away.

About CORA

"He sent the invitations when the party was over," Alistair Marsh of Bloomberg wrote of me in April 2019:[8]

> Only after the cryptocurrency craze's collapse hit bottom in December did Standard Chartered Plc veteran Hoe Lon Leng issue his call to the market's biggest traders: join him to brainstorm making digital tokens part of the world's financial architecture.
>
> It may seem quixotic, but the goal of the two dozen men gathered 20th January at a resort on Singapore's Sentosa Island was to create the framework for an orderly market in crypto derivatives—part of every primitive asset class's journey to acceptance. If they succeed, those hours spent in Sofitel meeting rooms hemmed in between an 18-hole golf course and one of the city-state's sandy beaches could prove to be a turning point, these true believers say.

The Amsterdam Stock Exchange is the oldest trading market in modern records. Founded by the Dutch East India Company in 1602, like all trading markets, it started with a few groups of people providing liquidity to each other. The motivation has always been to buy low and sell high, and players try to outwit each other through game theory, facilitating businesses from various clients and taking risks at the right time. Of course, the age-old problem is always going to be that someone will try to cheat, breaking the rules and regulations to get ahead.

How can we mitigate this problem in the new world of crypto? In January 2019, I got the idea of getting a large-scale gathering of over-the-counter (OTC) crypto traders for a sharing forum, to identify ways we could work together to improve the liquidity of the market, in other words, finding ways to make crypto a spendable currency rather than just a store of value.

Together with a former Standard Chartered colleague, Simon Nursey (now Head of Derivatives at QCP Capital), and lawyer Kenneth Oh from Dentons Rodyk, we held our meetings shortly before a large symposium at the Sofitel in Sentosa. We named it the Cryptocurrency OTC Roundtable Asia or CORA for short. Through CORA, the few of us hoped to gather the most critical players in the trading community, and collectively agree to do the right thing by establishing standards, clarifying key terms and ensuring a smooth marketplace.[9]

INTRODUCTION: WHEN GOOD PRODUCTS TURN BAD   23

CORA@Singapore

The group subsequently met in Chicago several months later, on 9 May 2019. Remember that those were dark days for the crypto market; Bitcoin and Ether had lost most of their value from their peak at $6,033 and $168, respectively. During market slumps, deflation pushes a lot of market players to sway away from professionalism. The CORA agenda then covered guidelines on dealing with scams and bad plays. We called for the setup of a "blacklist". As Marsh wrote:[10]

> The event, which drew traders from Singapore to San Francisco, highlighted the common will among the big players in crypto to impose standards from traditional finance on their immature market. It also made clear that there is much still to do to establish an ordered and trusted trading environment, especially in the over-the-counter derivatives contracts CORA is focused on.

CORA @ Chicago

What would turn out to be CORA's last meeting to date was held back at The Capella, Sentosa, in September 2019. With the "crypto winter" almost over, we had more participants than ever – and invited representatives from MAS and Blackrock to witness these relentless efforts to work together as an industry.

CORA @ The Capella

With firms like exchange Coinbase and crypto trading company Alameda Research now worth billions, and crypto itself going mainstream, some of the participants remain influential figures as I write today.

We're proud of what we accomplished and the direction we helped to set for the industry, the camaraderie, friendly competition and at times heated exchanges during the workgroup discussions have played a part in forming the basis of the markets today.

Your New Blocks
- All new technological trends follow a cycle of ups and downs as the world comes to terms with them. Each of these represents a new period of democratisation, as what was once available to only a few elites become cheap and simple enough for the masses to use.
- During these periods, there is still money to be made, more so from the winners that emerge.
- Blockchain remains a "solution in search of a problem." In other words, the race is on to find fields where its unique strengths can be applied.
- Don't speculate – take educated risks so scammers will find it harder to operate.

Endnotes

1 "Steam stops accepting payments in bitcoins", *BBC Technology*, 7 December 2017, at https://www.bbc.com/news/technology-42264622.

2 David Canellis, "FBI charges NiceHash founder over dangerous dark web malware (again)", *The Next Web*, 11 June 2019, at https://thenextweb.com/hardfork/2019/06/11/nicehash-fbi-mariposa-cryptocurrency-dark-web-malware-mining.

3 Julia Magas, "Bitcoin Not Accepted: Burger King's Crypto Foray Short-Lived", *CoinTelegraph*, 17 September 2019, at https://cointelegraph.com/news/bitcoin-not-accepted-burger-kings-crypto-foray-short-lived.

4 Jimmy Song, "Bitcoin's Path to Method of Payment", *Medium*, 4 September 2018, at https://medium.com/@jimmysong/bitcoins-path-to-method-of-payment-6cb5b3297268.

5 Stan Schroeder, "2018 was crypto's year of reckoning, but there's hope ahead", *Mashable*, 15 December 2018, at https://mashable.com/article/crypto-blockchain-year-in-review-2018.

6 "Gartner 2019 Hype Cycle Shows Most Blockchain Technologies Are Still Five to 10 Years Away From Transformational Impact", *Gartner*, 8 October 2019, at https://www.gartner.com/en/newsroom/press-releases/2019-10-08-gartner-2019-hype-cycle-shows-most-blockchain-technologies-are-still-five-to-10-years-away-from-transformational-impact.

7 "Uncharted territory: why consumers are still wary about adopting cryptocurrency – Kaspersky's Cryptocurrency Report 2019", *Kaspersky* (undated), at https://www.kaspersky.com/blog/cryptocurrency-report-2019.

8 Alistair Marsh, "Crypto's Long Road to Acceptance May Have Started Here", *Bloomberg*, 25 April 2019, at https://www.bloomberg.com/news/articles/2019-04-25/crypto-s-long-road-to-acceptance-may-have-started-here.

9 Frank Chaparro, "Crypto trading firms are under pressure, but a group is banding together to breathe new life into the OTC world", 3 May 2019, *Yahoo! Finance*, at https://finance.yahoo.com/news/crypto-trading-firms-under-pressure-201334015.html.

10 Alistair Marsh, "Crypto Traders Ponder Blacklist to Keep Scammers, Thieves at Bay", *Bloomberg*, 8 May 2019, at https://www.bloomberg.com/news/articles/2019-05-08/crypto-traders-ponder-blacklist-to-keep-scammers-thieves-at-bay.

PART I
A MATURING MARKET

Chapter 1

BUBBLE TROUBLE

"If you're the police, where are your badges?"

"Badges? We ain't got no badges. We don't need no badges. I don't have to show you any stinkin' badges!"
The Treasure of the Sierra Madre (1948)

What You'll Learn
- The truth about the blockchain and cryptocurrency crash of 2018.
- How blockchains have been attacked, compromised or otherwise failed, and are being improved.
- An update on ICOs and why they declined over 2018.

It was the end of 2017. Blockchains were now eight years old, the *Star Wars* movie *The Last Jedi* was irreparably dividing its fan community and Bitcoin had reached its all-time high. On 17 December, owners of bitcoins saw the value of each one rise to US$19,783.06, the highest it had ever been to date. Many commentators, including myself, were writing about how it would revolutionise the world of money, open up new avenues for banking and finance, and provide some of the world's most vulnerable people with a useful store of value.

It was during this time that the Chicago Options Exchange and Mercantile Exchange announced that they would open trading in future contracts for Bitcoin. Futures are a guard against increasing prices, in which assets like commodities or shares are bought "at a predetermined price at a specified time in the future".[1] In other words, these things are paid for when the contract expires, but at the price agreed upon earlier. Bitcoin traders hoped to capture a profit on the changing valuation of Bitcoin, by selling the futures contract at more than what they paid for it.

But trouble was brewing and, that same week, Swiss bank UBS warned:[2]

> We believe this has all the hallmarks of a bubble. High turnover, against limited real-world use, suggests that many buyers are seeking speculative gain. And while the supply of Bitcoins is limited, the broader stock of cryptocurrencies is not, with thousands of potential substitutes.

Markets, the bank warned, were in a "speculative bubble". It was certainly not a good time to invest in Bitcoin, as the markets "can remain irrational longer than you can remain solvent". The week saw the entire cryptocurrency market worth over US$600 billion. However, UBS was more open towards blockchain, the technology that Bitcoin and other cryptos are built on. Blockchain, the UBS report said, was expected to "generate USD 300bn–400bn of global economic value by 2027".

Early on, adopters were noting how volatile cryptocurrency was, preventing it from replacing fiat money for routine transactions. As expected, that high would not last, and just five days later, it fell to below $11,000. If you had bought some ten bitcoins earlier and sold them just a few days too late, you would have lost tens of thousands of dollars!

When Hackers Attack

Despite my reputation as an advisor to crypto projects and my belief in its eventual success, I must admit that blockchain technology has its share of teething problems, and has hardly been covered in glory. As the fledgling technology took off, hackers quickly realised its points of vulnerability and hit several exchanges and individuals. The scalps included Japan-based giant Mt Gox in 2014, the Ethereum network in 2016, Binance in 2019 and many users through ransomware demands.[3] (Note that this is *very* different from tampering with the Bitcoin protocol itself. But as we'll see, other cryptos haven't been so lucky.) Because Bitcoin's network is decentralised and no one party can declare a completed transaction invalid, the only way to get a refund is for the recipient to voluntarily send it back to you.

Fairly or not, Bitcoin had to shake off a reputation that it was merely another scam, or a tool for criminals. As PayPal founding CEO Bill Harris wrote in 2018:[4]

> In my opinion, it's a colossal pump-and-dump scheme, the likes of which the world has never seen. In a pump-and-dump game, promoters "pump" up the price of a security creating a speculative frenzy, then "dump" some of their holdings at artificially high prices. And some cryptocurrencies are pure frauds. ...
>
> Indeed, for the vast majority of uses, bitcoin has no role. Dollars, pounds, euros, yen and renminbi are better means of payment, stores of value and things in themselves.
>
> Cryptocurrency is best-suited for one use: Criminal activity. Because transactions can be anonymous – law enforcement cannot easily trace who buys and sells – its use is dominated by illegal endeavors.

Of course, just because cryptos or blockchain cannot do something now, it doesn't mean they will never be able to. Ethereum is built around the framework of automated software transactions called "smart contracts", in which agreements can be made to send ether tokens once certain conditions are met and coded into the network. As I wrote in *Decrypted*:[5]

> [Bitcoin pioneer Nick] Szabo was the first to spell out the possibility of computers automatically drawing up and executing transactions based on

simple, logical tests. He defined a smart contract as "a set of promises, specified in digital form, including protocols within which the parties perform on these promises."[6] This isn't a formal definition – there actually isn't one – but Ethereum co-founder [Vitalik] Butarin uses the following: "A smart contract is a computer program executed in a secure environment that directly controls digital assets."

In the context of blockchain, it can be adapted into: "… a computer program executed in a *blockchain* that directly controls *cryptocurrencies and tokens*."

In other words, a smart contract encodes an agreement between parties (and all supporting documents) in the form of a computer program, which will be executed once the agreed conditions are met. This agreement can be of any type – a loan, a transaction, an investment or anything else. Because it's on blockchain permanently, nothing can be deleted or lost. And due to the decentralised, trustless nature of blockchain, and the extreme difficulty of tampering with it, it's an excellent environment in which to carry out the outcome of the agreement.

But again, weaknesses were quickly found in this new approach, and in June 2016, a hacker took advantage of a smart contract loophole to siphon one-sixth of all the Ether in existence away. In a departure from the earlier philosophy of complete decentralisation, Ethereum's developers undid the theft by "rolling back" the network to the state it was in before, though not before gauging user support for the move. Those who disagreed with this move towards centralisation, and believed the network had worked exactly as designed, continued along the old rules with a new blockchain network known as Ethereum Classic.

Successful attacks, when they do happen, continue to make the news. *The Guardian* reported in July 2019:[7]

> Last year, Japan's Coincheck was hacked and more than $500m-worth of digital currency stolen. In 2017 the South Korean exchange Youbit shut down and filed for bankruptcy after being hacked twice. The Tokyo-based MtGox exchange, which at one time handled almost 80% of all global bitcoin transactions, was shut down in 2014 after 850,000 bitcoins (worth half a billion US dollars at the time) disappeared from its virtual vaults.

As recently as July 2019, Japan-based exchange Bitpoint became the latest high-profile victim, losing some US$32 million worth. To make matters worse, 51 per cent attacks against the very protocol of less in-demand cryptos have been more frequently successful.

Technology Review's Mike Orcutt described the underlying issue like this:[8]

> Susceptibility to 51% attacks is inherent to most cryptocurrencies. That's because most are based on blockchains that use proof of work as their protocol for verifying transactions. In this process, also known as mining, nodes spend vast amounts of computing power to prove themselves trustworthy enough to add information about new transactions to the database. A miner who somehow gains control of a majority of the network's mining power can defraud other users by sending them payments and then creating an alternative version of the blockchain in which the payments never happened.
>
> ...
>
> Toward the middle of 2018, attackers began springing 51% attacks on a series of relatively small, lightly traded coins including Verge, Monacoin, and Bitcoin Gold, stealing an estimated $20 million in total. In the fall, hackers stole around $100,000 using a series of attacks on a currency called Vertcoin. The hit against Ethereum Classic, which netted more than $1 million, was the first against a top-20 currency.

David Vorick, cofounder of the blockchain-based file storage platform Sia, predicts that 51% attacks will continue to grow in frequency and severity, and that exchanges will take the brunt of the damage caused by double-spends.

Orcutt pointed out that "hackers have stolen nearly $2 billion worth of cryptocurrency since the beginning of 2017, mostly from exchanges, and that's just what has been revealed publicly." It's now the case that the vulnerability of blockchains is directly tied to how much computing power is available to mine, and thus obtain the right to add to them. Bitcoin and Ether, due to the resources invested in them by the community over time, are for all practical purposes "safe" from 51 per cent attacks; less popular cryptos are not, a "club" whose unenviable membership now includes Ethereum Classic.

In sum, cryptocurrencies make attractive targets and have been attacked in various ways. Attackers can target the exchanges that trade them and hold them for customers by using traditional methods of social engineering and data theft; launching brute-force attacks and taking control of more than half the computing power used for mining them; or tampering with the coding of smart contracts themselves.

Perhaps even worse for cryptocurrencies, the public began seeing them as money there for the taking by any hacker intelligent enough. The underlying technology will only become more and more complex, creating new vulnerabilities and needing even more eyes on it – especially in the form of software engineers, government regulators and (perhaps most importantly of all) wise investors who know which problems are the result of cryptos themselves, and which come from a wider fluctuation in the stock market itself.

What hasn't helped is that hackers have grown even more sophisticated, targeting "bitcoin and cryptocurrency wallet information". At least one trojan (a malicious computer program disguised as a helpful one, named after the Trojan Horse) has been developed with the intention of finding crypto wallet information and delivering them to "a server controlled by the cyber criminals".

These are spread by users unwittingly downloading infected emails or applications. Even worse, another malware called Glupteba is being spread by online advertising scripts (a big reason not to click on online ads, whatever they promise) and is using the Bitcoin blockchain to update itself.[9] (This only affects infected machines that run the malware's own Bitcoin script, not every Bitcoin user.)

The arms race between cyber-security teams and hackers remains in full swing. As the Irish Republican Army warned Margaret Thatcher's British government after failing to assassinate her in 1984: "Today we were unlucky, but remember we only have to be lucky once. You will have to be lucky always."

ICOs: Good, Bad or Ugly?

In 2013, developer JR Willet proposed a way to build new protocols on top of Bitcoin's blockchain, using his protocol idea of Mastercoin as an intermediary. In the same White Paper, he also outlined a novel means of community fundraising. This early method involved creating what he called a "Trusted Entity":[10]

> ... an organization with a publicly known identity and location that would issue Mastercoins, coordinate the fundraising and distribute the funds for the protocol software development. From his other notes, it became obvious that this entity should not be controlled by developers and should have rather non-profit goals e.g. proliferation of the blockchain technology.

Notice that despite Bitcoin's decentralised nature, there was still no way to fully remove trust from the picture. Mastercoin pulled off what would come to be known as an Initial Coin Offering (ICO). Its vision would be more fully realised in Ethereum, and ICOs began to expand as a new way of raising money for the crypto projects that Ethereum and other similar frameworks promise to make possible. Because by design, anyone can create a new cryptocurrency, a firm launching an ICO can collect investor payments in the form of fiat currency or a token like Bitcoin or Ether, and in return, reward them with its own unique cryptocurrency token.

The company uses the invested money to pursue its goals and launch its product or service. If the company performs well, the implication is that these tokens will be worth much more in the future, providing the investors with a good return on investment. Because it is such a simple process, startups often turn to them as a means to bypass the strict process of fundraising through banks or venture capitalists.

The ICO entry in *Investopedia* pointed out the implications:[11]

> Investors buy into ICOs in the hope of quick and powerful returns on their investments. The most successful ICOs over the past several years give investors reason to maintain this hope, as they have indeed produced tremendous returns. However, this investor enthusiasm also leads people astray. Because they are largely unregulated, ICOs have become a hub of frauds and scam artists, looking to prey on investors who are overzealous and underinformed.

As I wrote in my earlier book, *Decrypted*, the government cannot ignore the presence of a means of doing commerce that bypasses its hold on fiat money. Regulations, or the threat of bans and restrictions, have also influenced investor behaviour and disrupted the value of the cryptos themselves.

The year 2018 proved to be crypto's worst to date. Over the course of the year, nearly $700 billion in crypto valuation would be lost. Companies worth millions of dollars could lose it all practically overnight, and my own partners and advisory clients weren't spared.

Bitcoin's price went into what Fox Business calls "freefall" in 2018.[12] As government scrutiny increased, technology giants Google and Facebook banned advertising for ICOs and cryptocurrencies, and the United States' Security and Exchange Commission stopped a prediction I and many others have made from coming true – cryptocurrency-based exchange traded funds or ETFs. I do understand their concerns, as the ICO landscape is still rife with scams, poor teamwork or just plain unrealistic ideas.

In the absence of a widespread, viable product on par with traditional business models, blockchain startups must rely on the expertise of their team members, a minimum viable product, buzz created by their projects ... and faith in blockchain itself as a problem-solving technology for the future.

"Unfortunately for those at the time who were betting on more immediate upside, one of bitcoin's many speculative bubbles or 'hype cycles' reached its peak on Dec. 17, 2017 and its price has been trapped in a steep and record-setting downtrend ever since," wrote *Coindesk*'s Sam Ouimet on 2 January 2019.[13]

What differentiated this downtrend from previous ones was the long-term trend of steady decline. Its price entered a zone when "a major short-term moving average crosses below a major long-term moving average, indicating a significant loss of strength to the longer term trend." In other words, the price has entered a bearish zone for the long term, and is unlikely to recover. This is known as a "death cross", hardly a term to inspire confidence.[14]

Bitcoin plunged to just above $3,000 at the end of 2018, a depreciation of more than 70 per cent. When Bitcoin falls, for better or worse it's a reflection of crypto in general, so everyone issuing it was facing that decline as well. An amount of $40 million in bitcoins or ether might turn into 30, 20, 10 or even 5. I personally saw Kyber's valuation fall from a few hundred million dollars to just tens. Zilliqa, the famous Singapore-launched crypto, was at $1.5 billion valuation, but during this "crypto winter" it plunged to less than $100 million at one point. As I write, it is stronger than ever, with more adoptions and a market cap above $2 billion.

But some cryptos have reached zero, or even gone out of business. In traditional IPOs, there is protection as some kind of price stabilisation must be planned – it's something an ethical employer would do with the available funds. Your investors must know that there is a plan to stabilise your coins, because if literally no one is interested, that's an immediate valuation of zero.

If anything, this is where a traditional means of price stabilisation from the traditional financial world can (and should) come in. According to *Investopedia*, one such mechanism is known as a stabilizing bid:[15]

> A stabilizing bid is a purchase of stock by underwriters to stabilize, or support, the secondary market price of a security immediately following an initial public offering (IPO) when the price of the newly issued shares falters or is shaky in trading.

...

After a company has made a decision to go public, it will vet a number of underwriters for expertise in valuing the company's equity, marketing and distribution, sell-side research support, and trading functions. The risk of negative perception of the company is high should the trading price fall below the IPO price. To prepare for this risk, the issuer grants the underwriters a greenshoe option, otherwise known as an overallotment option, that allows the underwriters to oversell or short up to 15% more shares than initially offered by the company. If demand does, in fact, begin to look weak and the price wavers out of the gate, the underwriters will step in with a stabilizing bid by buying back the shorted shares. This demand source from the underwriters for the newly-issued shares will help to shore up, or stabilize, the stock price.

IPOs have used these safeguards for many years. In part, ICOs were established to get around those requirements, theoretically saving time and paperwork. But that left many without protection from volatility and falling prices, exactly the things Bitcoin (and by extension, Ethereum and their own tokens) were vulnerable to.

Even worse, I've found that too many companies simply dumped and ran, shutting down or going silent rather than face the repercussions. Many ICOs have indeed been run by young blockchain pioneers, but youth and inexperience in this case work against them – they have not had the experience of weathering such a crisis before. Some try to keep the company running, even if they must scrap the entire timeline and start over; others pocket investors' money and close shop, while another group completely vanish off the grid. All these things have happened, and this number is not even counting the number of ICOs that were scams to begin with.

(Note that not every failed ICO or company is a scam. I believe the word should only be used to mean a *deliberate* attempt to mislead investors; that is, there needs to be both the intent and the ability to do so. This is why I'm hesitant to use the word on a specific company, it must go out of its way to earn the label.)

Fortunately, Bitcoin's price has rallied and from March to July 2019, it recovered, and as I write in October 2019, it now stands at just above $8,000, dropping by one-third from a high of just over $12,700. It could be argued that the "bubble" has been a net *good* for cryptos in general, because it filters out the scams and bad ideas, far more quickly than bubbles of the past. Perhaps the crypto collapse has served, as Channel NewsAsia's Janice Lim puts it, as the "reality check" the industry needs.[16]

The figures are sobering. Crypto investors have seen their portfolios shrink dramatically, and Singapore's exchanges have reported declining trading volume over 2018's bear market. "When it's a bull market, everybody wanted to jump into Bitcoin. Now, they are not so eager to get in because they don't know where the market is going," says Rune Evensen of exchange COSS.

Hardware sales also petered out, and many stores selling mining rigs have had orders shrink from hundreds of thousands of dollars every month to practically nothing.

The Problem of Hype

I don't know how many scammers will eventually be caught, but they have indeed retarded the mainstream adoption of cryptos as a value store, as opposed to more traditional instruments like stocks and bonds. An ETF equivalent of cryptos hasn't come yet, and much as we may not like to admit it, for good reason. Perhaps a warning from the 19th-century writer GK Chesterton said it best:[17]

> There exists in such a case a certain institution or law; let us say, for the sake of simplicity, a fence or gate erected across a road. The more modern type of reformer goes gaily up to it and says, "I don't see the use of this; let us clear it away." To which the more intelligent type of reformer will do well to answer: "If you don't see the use of it, I certainly won't let you clear it away. Go away and think. Then, when you can come back and tell me that you do see the use of it, I may allow you to destroy it."

This chapter has so far focused on just one use of blockchains: to power cryptocurrencies like Bitcoin. It has many more uses in the same way that the Internet can be used for more than just email ... but what *are* those uses, exactly?

Yessi Bello Perez of *The Next Web* pointed out the root problem behind the crash – *hype*. Because we simply don't know the answer to that question yet, many pioneer companies are exploring various ways blockchain can be used to improve things. Perhaps the very ease of open source P2P networking, as was built into Bitcoin from the beginning, gave off encouraging signals that the technology could be applied nearly anywhere, but would it be better than what we already have?

Ultimately, we're learning the root cause of many problems for investors is that too often, that area *did not* need the advantages that blockchain could bring. "[It's] fair to say the industry has matured somewhat, but the rhetoric remains largely the same," she says.[18] The promises of better transparency and efficiency are still there, but does that sector even need it, when its existing checks and balances work well enough?

At this point, we're entering a phase where we need to be more realistic about our expectations, and that includes understanding how to calibrate them. If there is indeed a real need for blockchain, we need some ways to think about how best to find it and apply blockchain as a solution.

Your New Blocks
- Warnings of cryptos being a bubble came early, but investors needed to heed that advice in line with the changes that were coming to the market, and not panic.
- Many ICOs and other coin projects have failed due to excessive hype; which means we need to be more selective about what projects we back, and how.

- Some limits are needed on the growth of crypto, so that investors and companies can work in a safe, well-regulated environment.

Endnotes

1 James Chen (reviewer), "Futures Contract", *Investopedia*, 1 April 2019, at https://www.investopedia.com/terms/f/futurescontract.asp.

2 Oscar Williams-Grut, "UBS: Bitcoin 'has all the hallmarks of a bubble'", *Business Insider*, 21 December 2017, at https://www.businessinsider.sg/ubs-bitcoin-bubble-2017-12/?r=UK.

3 "Mt Gox" is literally pronounced "Em-tee Gox". It began as a network for trading *Magic: the Gathering* game cards online, hence the acronym MTGOX, for "*Magic: the Gathering* Online Exchange".

4 Bill Harris, "Bitcoin is the greatest scam in history", *Vox Recode*, 24 April 2018, at https://www.vox.com/2018/4/24/17275202/bitcoin-scam-cryptocurrency-mining-pump-dump-fraud-ico-value.

5 Leng Hoe Lon, *Decrypted* (Marshall Cavendish Business, 2019) p 68.

6 For more on Szabo and his pioneering work, see Michael Gord, "Smart Contracts Described by Nick Szabo 20 Years Ago Now Becoming Reality", *Bitcoin Magazine*, 26 April 2016, at https://bitcoinmagazine.com/articles/smart-contracts-described-by-nick-szabo-years-ago-now-becoming-reality-1461693751.

7 Shane Hickey, "$32m stolen from Tokyo cryptocurrency exchange in latest hack", *The Guardian*, 12 July 2019, at https://www.theguardian.com/technology/2019/jul/12/tokyo-cryptocurrency-exchange-hack-bitpoint-bitcoin.

8 Mike Orcutt, "Once hailed as unhackable, blockchains are now getting hacked", *MIT Technology Review*, 19 February 2019, at https://www.technologyreview.com/s/612974/once-hailed-as-unhackable-blockchains-are-now-getting-hacked. A double-spend is the problem cryptocurrencies were developed to solve – a trusted authority needs to verify that when Isaac transfers some money to Ling, both parties are who they say they are, and that once Ling has received the money, Isaac is no longer in possession of it. In other words, the same unit of money cannot be spent twice.

9 Billy Bambrough, "Warning Issued After Malware Is Found To Have Hijacked Bitcoin Blockchain", *Forbes*, 7 September 2019, at https://www.forbes.com/sites/billybambrough/2019/09/07/serious-malware-warning-over-bitcoin-blockchain/#2d581f6b7c28.

10 Ivona Skultetyova, "Short History of ICOs: From Crypto Experiment to Revolution in Startup Financing", ehvLINC, 3 February 2018, at https:// medium.com/@ehvLINC/short-history-of-icos-from-crypto-experiment-to-revolution-in-startup-financing-709c23839ffc.

11 Jake Frankenfield (reviewer), "Initial Coin Offering (ICO)", *Investopedia*, 20 December 2018, at https://www.investopedia.com/terms/i/initial-coin-offering-ico.asp.

12 Thomas Barrabi, "Bitcoin hits $11K: A timeline of cryptocurrency's rise, fall and rebound", Fox Business, 24 June 2019, at https://www.foxbusiness.com/markets/bitcoin-price-history-timeline-cryptocurrency.

13 Sam Ouimet, "Down More than 70% in 2018, Bitcoin Closes Its Worst Year on Record", *Coindesk*, 2 January 2019, at https://www.coindesk.com/down-more-than-70-in-2018-bitcoin-closes-its-worst-year-on-record.

14 According to *Investopedia*, "A moving average (MA) is a widely used indicator in technical analysis that helps smooth out price action by filtering out the 'noise' from random short-term price fluctuations." See Adam Hayes (reviewer), "Moving Average", *Investopedia*, 19 June 2019, at https://www.investopedia.com/terms/m/movingaverage.asp.

15 Will Kenton (reviewer), "Stabilizing Bid," *Investopedia*, 21 June 2019, at https://www.investopedia.com/terms/s/stabilizingbid.asp.

16 Janice Lim, "The Big Read: Cryptocurrency crash offers industry the reality check it needs", *Channel NewsAsia*, 10 December 2018, at https://www.channelnewsasia.com/news/singapore/the-big-read-cryptocurrency-crash-offers-industry-the-reality-11015242.

17 GK Chesterton, *The Thing: Why I Am a Catholic* (Dodd, Mead & Co, 1930).

18 Yessi Bello Perez, "Hype is killing blockchain technology", *The Next Web*, 7 February 2019, at https://thenextweb.com/hardfork/2019/02/07/why-hype-is-killing-blockchain-technology.

Chapter 2

THESE TURBULENT COINS: WHY CRYPTO IS HERE TO STAY

> It's good to have people talk about it because the more they talk about it, the more they realize how important bitcoin is going to be for the planet, for all of us.
> **Tim Draper**[1]

What You'll Learn
- How fears of government action have led to panic and uncertainty.
- Why many of these fears are unwarranted, and how to approach impending new regulation.
- Why crypto is still going strong, and how the concept can still be a good investment in the future.

One of the perils of being a leader, as faced by the more popular and influential of leaders, is how one's words are interpreted. Even a casual remark or light-hearted joke may be taken literally. As recounted by Singapore architect Khew Sin Khoon, founding Prime Minister Lee Kuan Yew, while being driven past Khew's university hostel in 1983, commented that a tree had been planted "too close to the building, and that its roots may damage the foundation."

The tree was gone the very next day. "I later found out that the University's Estate Office had an overzealous staff who interpreted Mr Lee's comment as an instruction to remove the tree!" Khew wrote. "Such was the power of Lee Kuan Yew's words, and the actions that followed."[2]

The principle remains the same whether the subject is a tree, an entire parallel legal system or a newly created financial product, and this was a lesson that King Henry II of England learnt and paid for in blood. As a young prince, he had become friends with Thomas Becket, the son of a London textile merchant. Despite the differences in their station and age (Becket was more than a decade older), they became inseparable. They spent much of their free time together, and "people said the two men 'had but one heart and one mind'."[3]

Henry ascended the throne in 1154 at the age of 21, and appointed Becket his Lord Chancellor the next year. The two worked together to enforce law and order, and collected debts owed to the throne. Becket proved so capable that Henry saw in him a way to bring the formidable Church of England to heel. "Any action against the Church was certain to bring divine punishment against the guilty person and his people – even if that action was taken by a king," as noted in a *BBC Bitesize* article.[4]

In those days, the Church was far more powerful politically than its modern incarnation. Despite being nominally loyal to the Crown, in practice the Church had its own court and laws, and answered to the Pope in Rome.⁵ As Ben Johnson pointed out in a *Historic UK* article:⁶

> Priests who murdered or raped could avoid common-law justice by claiming 'benefit of clergy', the right to be tried in the bishop's court. The worst that could happen here was to be issued with a severe penance or exceptionally, expulsion (defrocking) from the priesthood.

In other words, clergy were held to be above English secular law. Even lower-ranking clergy had this privilege, and Henry felt it undercut the authority of the Crown in enforcement of the law. "Because even those men who took minor orders were considered clerks (clerics), the quarrel over the so-called 'criminous clerks' potentially covered up to one-fifth of the male population of England", noted a *History Hit* article.⁷ Indeed, to this day Henry is known as the father of common law – the concept of legal principles being derived from precedent court decisions, rather than being written down as legislation.

When Archbishop Theobald of Canterbury died in 1161, Henry took the chance to appoint his friend to the top position in the Church, hoping that Becket would take his side and place the Church's vast holdings and clergy under royal supremacy. Becket was ordained as a priest in June 1162, and installed as the new Archbishop of Canterbury the very next day.

However, shortly after his consecration, a dramatic change came over the new archbishop. He gave up the high life he was accustomed to, resigned from his post as Lord Chancellor, and became an ascetic immersed in godly activities. It was said that his only garment from that point on was a filthy hair shirt. More importantly, Becket began actively championing the Church's rights *against* his friend, the King. The two clashed over not only the legal rights of the clergy, but the authority to confiscate lands that the Archdiocese of Canterbury had previously lost.

By 1163, any friendship between the two had effectively broken down. Henry dismissed Becket from royal favour, and the next year was spent manoeuvring for political advantage and gathering allies in France, the Holy Roman Empire and Rome itself. The two would meet in January 1164 at Clarendon Palace, when Henry threatened the bishops with severe penalties unless they joined him, weakened their ties to Rome and gave up the right to appeal their sentences to the Pope. Becket was issued an additional demand to account for all the monies he had handled as Lord Chancellor. Under duress, Becket agreed to the King's demands, but he had read between the lines and knew Henry was now his enemy.

Becket fled to France, and both parties wrote to various authorities requesting their support. He was to remain in exile until 1170, when the King crowned his son Henry (known as the "Young King") as co-ruler at Westminster Abbey. The coronation was performed by Archbishop Roger of York, instead of Becket as was his traditional duty as Archbishop of Canterbury.

This incident forced Pope Alexander III's hand against King Henry, and the threat of papal censure had the King reopening negotiations with Becket. Eventually, Henry had to give up his quest to reduce the power of the Church, and in December 1170, Becket returned to England. However, in doing so, Becket excommunicated several of his fellow bishops (including Roger of York) whom he deemed too supportive of the King, opening a new political rift. In frustration, shortly after Christmas, Henry shouted to his court the words he is best remembered for: "Will no one rid me of this turbulent priest?"[8]

While not expressed as an order, the words were taken in that spirit by four knights who overheard him, and secretly travelled to Canterbury Cathedral to apprehend Becket. It is said that as they confronted Becket, he told them, "If all the swords in England were pointed against my head, your threats would not move me. I am ready to die for my Lord, that in my blood the Church may obtain liberty and peace."

Seeing his refusal, the knights tried to apprehend him by force. Whether they truly wanted to assassinate him is unknown, but whatever their intentions, the archbishop resisted being dragged from his cathedral. "Touch me not, Reginald!" he retorted to one of them. "You and your accomplices act like madmen!"

Angered, the knights drew their swords and cut Becket down in front of his horrified monks.

Becket was one of the most popular men in England at the time of his death, and Henry's reputation was ruined. It provided the Church and the ordinary people with a martyr to rally around, and Henry lost his own favour with the Catholic Church, which he desperately needed at a time of rebellion by his own sons, John and Richard (later known as "the Lionheart").

In a reconciliation process called the Compromise of Avranches, Henry was absolved of any guilt for Becket's murder, on condition that he repealed the Clarendon laws and publicly showed he was sorry. In 1174, he did so by walking barefoot to Becket's tomb, allowing the monks to whip him along the way. The four assassins themselves were sentenced and sent by Rome to the Holy Land on crusade for 14 years.

But what does all this history have to do with cryptocurrencies, tokens and ICOs? Simply this: like the Church and its parallel legal system, cryptocurrencies and tokens form a parallel economic system that cannot be wished away. The point of this narrative is not to judge whether having such a parallel system is right or wrong, merely to show that they can and often do arise, and the words of leaders have an outsized impact on the established and new orders alike.

The crash in their values were largely brought about by the interpretation of Asian ministers' words, rightly or wrongly, in the same way that the four knights had done so with Henry's presumably rhetorical question nearly a millennium before. Henry could not simply have Becket arrested or killed, in the same way governments cannot slap a blanket ban on cryptocurrencies and jail anyone possessing them. Like it or not, they are too entrenched in financial markets and millions of people's wallets to be outlawed.

Uncertainty – Good or Bad?

By early January 2018, rumours began to spread that South Korea, home to some of the most enthusiastic adopters of Bitcoin, would ban trading in cryptocurrencies altogether, after a ban on domestic ICOs in 2017. Pouring fuel on the fire, Justice Minister Park Sang-ki announced that the rumours stemmed from truth – the ministry was "basically preparing a bill to ban cryptocurrency trading through exchanges."[9] South Korea is a major crypto trading market, and such statements from its leaders are taken very seriously. In the end, what the country banned was anonymous bank account use in trading crypto.[10]

Major cryptos, like Bitcoin, Ethereum, Ripple and more had hit record highs earlier, but now "took a hammering" as the news spread. "Will no one rid us of these turbulent coins?" the Korean government seemed to be demanding, as the Chinese had done in September 2017 by temporarily banning ICOs.[11] The same impulse that led to the knights murdering Becket would kick off the worst loss of cryptocurrencies' value in their short history, and *minutes* later, over $106 billion had been lost from the entire crypto market. "Koreans reacted by petitioning the authorities to go easy", noted *Quartz*'s Devjyot Ghoshal.[12] One plea spoke of cryptocurrencies as the source of a "happy dream", and of one day being able to afford a house and "a life of doing something I want to do."

"In terms of cryptocurrencies, generally, I can say with almost certainty that they will come to a bad ending. When it happens or how or anything else, I don't know," Berkshire Hathaway's Warren Buffett told CNBC. "If I could buy a five-year put on every one of the cryptocurrencies, I'd be glad to do it but I would never short a dime's worth."[13] (A "put" is an options contract that gives its owner the right to sell the underlying stock at the price set at the time, not the price it will be worth at sale, within a specific time period.) In other words, Buffett is far more comfortable betting on short-term fluctuations in the value of cryptocurrencies than he is about them as a store of value into the future.

Buffett's right-hand man Charlie Munger was even less optimistic, calling Bitcoin and venture capital funding of blockchain startups "bubbles" that would end badly.[14] If anything, the battle lines were now clearer than ever, with financiers and investors taking sides in what was becoming a polarised debate.

I still stand by my predictions and high hopes for blockchain technology, even if they take more time to implement than once thought. If it sounds like I'm being too negative, it's not because I don't want to see cryptocurrencies and blockchains succeed, it's because I firmly believe this can only happen if we're honest and transparent about their weaknesses. Governments will have to contend with the reality of cryptos, and new entrants like Mark Zuckerberg, with his Facebook-anchored Libra cryptocurrency (now known as Diem), have far more power to maintain more disruptive parallel systems than Thomas Becket ever did.

If that means more volatility and uncertainty in the short term, that's to be expected as part of the introduction of any pioneering new technology. The year 2018 was the worst for crypto to date, but it remains to be seen how much was due to crypto's shortcomings, and how much to a bearish stock market in general – one not helped by talk of a trade war between the United States and China. The crypto decline has to be seen in the context of the entire stock market and macro economy; for instance, equities rose in January and crashed down in February, and stabilised for the middle part of the year ... before crashing back down in December.

The downturn affected more than 90 per cent of all tradeable assets, and it would be very unusual if crypto were any different. Remember, at this point, it is more of a stock-like financial product than it is a spendable, liquid currency on the level of fiat money.

Yet, even in South Korea, there is promise. Many blockchain-based firms have emerged from the country, and the Korean government has looked favourably on projects like messaging app Kakao's Ground X initiative, and ICON, a holding of investment fund Hashed. Perhaps the crypto mania has had the longer-term effect of creating awareness of the uses of blockchain as a technological tool, rather than simply cryptocurrencies as a store of value. It will, however, take time for these to filter down to the point where they change the lives of ordinary people for the better.

ICOs are Dead – Long Live ICOs

The ICO is dying. I don't think there's any sugar-coating the news that this fundraising method is over and done with, at least in its current form. According to *Bitcoinist*, ICO projects are declining both in number and success rate, from over 100 each month in January 2018 "to almost nothing". The projected total take for ICOs is projected at a mere $338 million, just a twentieth of 2018's total. Researchers at LongHash concluded: "It wouldn't be a surprise to see the ICO model vanish completely in 2020."[15]

I've consulted on and run ICOs myself, and have come to a new understanding of their use. Compared to IPOs, it's hard to see how they can survive in a world where the model itself has become associated with scandal and failure. An ICO doesn't even give you a tangible stake in a company, or any kind of equity; unlike taking part in an IPO, which grants you a more traditional, protected share of a company. Being a shareholder means your investment is working to provide the company with some kind of governance, with the promise that your shares will be worth more in the future.

That means the value of a coin is always going to be vulnerable to speculation. As I've repeated throughout and no doubt will again, the bottom line is never to invest what you can't afford to lose, and keep borrowed money to a minimum. That's why I cautioned in *Decrypted*:[16]

> Much remains unknown, so treat ICO trading like you would the stock of a risky startup. Maybe it will succeed; maybe it won't. Don't ignore ICOs completely, but don't give in to greed, or invest so much you lose sleep over what might happen.

But I don't believe the ICO model is dying – it's merely evolving, and this will be the subject of the next chapter. Meanwhile, here are the five reasons why I would still back cryptos and blockchain firms, although wisely and cautiously:

1. *It's too early to tell what their long-term impact will be.* Blockchain is growing in popularity, and the fact that new

uses for digital tokens are being found points to their utility in the future. As we'll see, a digitised token allows you to partially own something that is traditionally thought of as indivisible, like a house or a car.
2. *Weaknesses will be discovered – that's how every industry has learnt and grown.* No new technology springs forth fully formed, and blockchain is no exception. Instead, growth is achieved through careful, repeated iteration and discovery of what works and what doesn't. It's not enough to find a weakness, it must be transparently studied, discussed and resolved.
3. *Knowing weaknesses helps developers and investors strategically strengthen weak points.* Knowledgeable investors are more important than ever. Blockchain's press is a good thing in that an educated base of supporters and users can target their investments wisely, and support those projects that truly solve problems in a feasible way.
4. *Successful implementation of blockchain and cryptocurrency remains a net good.* In my previous book, I talked about Bitcoin being "money without borders". In places where markets are inaccessible due to mismanagement, natural disaster or other causes, blockchain might yet save lives by providing transparent financial services and decentralised delivery to the worst-hit areas through smart contracts and autonomous vehicles. It must be stressed, however, that it is only a tool – its users will determine the results.
5. *By front-loading the work, we pave the way for easier future success.* The first companies to achieve viable products and services that perform better than traditional models will

be rightly hailed as pioneers in a new world of business. It will be easier than ever for other companies to replicate their success once this happens.

Imagine, if you will, investing in the Ford Motor Company in its earliest years when cars were still a novelty and the infrastructure to support them had not yet been built. It's indeed true that horses and carriages were still more convenient, but their days were numbered as automobile technology continued to improve and a network of roads, gas stations and other support facilities became available.

The downturns we've seen aren't the market collapsing or being regulated out of existence. It's the ecosystem maturing and learning more about what can or cannot be done. If you feel burned out and want to exit crypto for a while, I completely understand, though as we'll see, it's hardly the death knell ... any more than the dot-com bubble was.

Your New Blocks
- Leaders, both in the political and business spheres, have an outsized influence on public and employee perceptions, and therefore on the value of any stock or token. Step back and consider various points of view, including how markets have recovered in the past.
- Cryptos and blockchain tokens are similar to other financial products in many ways. Much of what we think is a "crypto bubble" actually coincides with deeper problems that affect other markets as well.

- Crypto and blockchain startups aren't dying out, but improving and growing as they work the problems out of their business models.

Endnotes

1 Jesse Pound, "Silicon Valley's Tim Draper, wearing a bitcoin tie, says crypto coins are good for humanity", CNBC, 19 July 2019, at https://www.cnbc.com/2019/07/19/tim-draper-says-cryptocurrencies-bitcoin-are-good-for-humanity.html.

2 Khew Sin Khoon, "In Memory of Lee Kuan Yew (1923–2015)", *Butterfly Circle*, 28 March 2015, at http://butterflycircle.blogspot.com/2015/03/in-memory-of-lee-kuan-yew-1923-2015.html.

3 Ben Johnson, "Thomas Becket: Murder in the Cathedral", *Historic UK* (undated), at https://www.historic-uk.com/HistoryUK/HistoryofEngland/Thomas-Becket.

4 "Thomas Becket and Henry II", *BBC Bitesize* (undated), at https://www.bbc.co.uk/bitesize/guides/zw3wxnb/revision/1.

5 This was before the Protestant Reformation four centuries later, when King Henry VIII pulled the Church of England away from Rome and asserted his own authority over it.

6 Ben Johnson, "Thomas Becket: Murder in the Cathedral", *Historic UK* (undated), at https://www.historic-uk.com/HistoryUK/HistoryofEngland/Thomas-Becket.

7 "How Falling Out with Henry II Resulted in Thomas Becket's Slaughter", *History Hit*, 31 July 2018, at https://www.historyhit.com/how-falling-out-with-henry-ii-resulted-in-thomas-beckets-slaughter.

8 There is some disagreement over the words themselves. One of Becket's monks renders them: "What miserable drones and traitors have I nourished and brought up in my household, who let their lord be treated with such shameful contempt by a low-born cleric?"

9 Arjun Kharpal, "Over $100 billion wiped off global cryptocurrency market following talk of South Korea trading ban", CNBC, 11 January 2018, at https://www.cnbc.com/2018/01/11/bitcoin-ripple-ethereum-prices-fall-after-south-korea-trading-ban-talk.html.

10 Yogita Khatri, "South Korea Will Maintain ICO Ban After Finding Token Projects Broke Rules", *Coindesk*, 31 January 2019, at https://www.coindesk.com/south-korea-will-maintain-ico-ban-after-finding-token-projects-broke-rules.

11 For the response to the temporary Chinese ban in September 2017, see Joseph Hincks, "Virtually Every Cryptocurrency in the World Is Tanking Right Now", *Time*, 5 September 2017, at https://time.com/4926712/cryptocurrency-crash-bitcoin-ethereum-ether-investing-ripple.

12 Devjyot Ghoshal, "South Korea's crypto craze has morphed into a blockchain boom", *Quartz*, 22 December 2018, at https://qz.com/1485034/how-south-koreas-crypto-craze-turned-into-a-blockchain-boom.

13 Berkeley Lovelace Jr, "Buffett on cryptocurrencies: 'I can say almost with certainty that they will come to a bad ending'", CNBC, 10 January 2018, at https://www.cnbc.com/2018/01/10/buffett-says-cyrptocurrencies-will-almost-certainly-end-badly.html.

14 Tae Kim, "Buffett partner Charlie Munger says bitcoin, Silicon Valley are bubbles," CNBC, 10 January 2018, at https://www.cnbc.com/2018/01/10/buffett-partner-charlie-munger-says-bitcoin-silicon-valley-are-bubbles.html. Munger has been against Bitcoin from the beginning, calling it "total insanity" and suggesting he would avoid it "like the plague".

15 Anja van Oosterhout, "ICOs 'Will Disappear in 2020' as Data Shows 95% Funding Decline", *Bitcoinist*, 3 October 2019, at https://bitcoinist.com/icos-will-disappear-in-2020-as-data-shows-95-funding-decline.

16 Leng Hoe Lon, *Decrypted* (Marshall Cavendish Business, 2019) p 87.

Chapter 3

THE EMERGING NEW MARKET

> The most important point is what value will every participant get out of permissioned blockchains, and candidly, I will love the day when nobody talks about blockchain and they just talk about the value creation.
>
> Marie Wieck, IBM blockchain general manager

What You'll Learn
- The ways the market has adapted in light of the high rate of ICO scams and failures.
- The trends to look out for as the crypto market enters a new phase.
- The advent of Stablecoin and how this differs from cryptocurrencies as we know them.

One of the strangest business pivots in history took place in December 2017. The company behind Long Island Iced Tea used the three magic words that can be relied on to shoot stock prices up – they announced they were about to "pivot to blockchain".

Learning that other companies had achieved massive valuation increases simply by adding "blockchain" to their name, Long Island did the same. The press release contained all the right buzzwords: "building blockchain infrastructure" and "new smart contract platform". To be fair, it did not promise results – then CEO Philip Thomas only said he would build "a world-class team of industry professionals" and "[pursue] our new direction in a thoughtful and deliberate manner."[1]

So far, so good. But what many missed out was that Long Island had endured a rocky first listing on Nasdaq, and was in danger of being delisted altogether early on. Its stock offering fell short of expectations (netting only $6.9 million instead of the expected $10 million), and prices fell on the first trading day. Its market value remained too low to remain on Nasdaq, and it had "until April 2018 to fix the situation".

Magical Words, Magical Thinking

Blockchain was in a unique place in 2017. It was widespread enough to be taken seriously as a financial product; available enough through the open-source nature of Bitcoin; yet little-understood enough that speculators were betting on any company that claimed to harness it. That claim (and a name change to Long Blockchain) was precisely what was needed to increase Long Island's share prices by a whopping *300 per cent*. It even reserved the Internet domain "www.longblockchain.com", and requested that Nasdaq change its trading symbol from LTEA to LBCC.

In January 2018, the Securities and Exchange Commission (SEC) had had enough. Chairman Jay Clayton warned:[2]

> I doubt anyone in this audience thinks it would be acceptable for a public company with no meaningful track record in pursuing the commercialization of distributed ledger or blockchain technology to (1) start to dabble in blockchain activities, (2) change its name to something like "Blockchain-R-Us," and (3) immediately offer securities, without providing adequate disclosure to Main Street investors about those changes and the risks involved.

In other words, talk is cheap. Over the beginning of 2018, Long Island explored, then abandoned, various blockchain deals and partnerships. It was noted in the *CoinTelegraph* article that Nasdaq eventually delisted the company, and in September, the SEC subpoenaed it. By July 2019, the company's executives were still under federal investigation – it turned out that the FBI had grown suspicious of how similar this was to a "pump and dump" scheme, and was "hunting for evidence of insider trading and securities fraud."[3]

A recent *Dilbert* comic strip captures the absurdity of many blockchain efforts by companies.[4] The CEO of Dilbert's company doesn't understand why the Pointy-Haired Boss is recommending blockchain, and the explanation by the boss doesn't make any sense: "You see, using blockchain is like losing a necklace on the beach," he says. "Then a seagull finds the necklace and takes it back to its nest. And we all like data security, don't we?"

"It's almost as if you're proposing a plan you don't understand at any level," the CEO replies.

It's as if cartoonist Scott Adams has put his finger on a large part of the market which is stabilising against the high price that Bitcoin once fetched, and now commands a lower price that is more in line with reality. An obstacle to that happening has been a general ignorance of how blockchain works, what it can realistically be used for, and the more down-to-earth but still secure and powerful alternatives. After all, if an existing solution and a radically new one could solve the same problem, why go with the one still in its infancy?

If 2017 was the year that promises were being made, then 2018 was the year that sifted out those that had a chance of coming true. The years 2019 and 2020 became a season of refinement, new beginnings and a clearer understanding of the technology behind blockchain. Hopefully, investors, VCs and government policy-makers alike will be better informed than the Pointy-Haired Boss.

The important thing to note about new technology is that because so much remains unknown, we simply have no idea what to expect. We saw an early euphoria precisely because the oceans of possibility were stretching out before us. Today, as we dive in, paddle around and explore, we're seeing that the depths are far more treacherous than we thought, and we have to find ways to mitigate them and navigate in safety. What we're seeing today is simply the world adjusting to the complex new realities blockchain has set up. And if we all agreed on how to do it, Bitcoin would still be the only blockchain in existence!

Instead, we're seeing more problem-solving and forking of blockchains to achieve various needs. Some will succeed, many will fail – but manage failure well, and it is but a stepping stone to eventual success.

Stocks, Coins and Derivatives

It is said that in ancient times, the Phoenician philosopher Thalus "forecast[ed] the next olive harvest would be an exceptionally good one."[5] The story is told by Aristotle, and preserved today in Professor Stephen G Cecchetti's textbook, *Derivatives for Decision Makers:*[6]

> As a poor philosopher, he did not have many financial resources at hand. But he used what he had to place a deposit on the local olive presses. As nobody knew for certain whether the harvest would be good or bad, Thalus secured the rights to the presses at a relatively low rate. When the harvest proved to be bountiful, and so demand for the presses was high, Thalus charged a high price for their use and reaped a considerable profit.

Thalus' deposit "gave him the right but not the obligation to hire the press", as noted in the book. "If the harvest had failed, his losses were limited to the initial deposit he paid." In other words, Thalus had purchased an option.

Today, options are but one choice we have from the family of financial instruments known as derivatives, and I see cryptocurrencies becoming the next "olives" with which to buy options. The underlying instrument has a certain value, and the derivatives built up around it have a price *derived* from the value of that instrument. Options trading has emerged as a way to mitigate risks or obtain leverage.

How does it work? If in December 2019, Bitcoin is at $12,000, Manash can either buy one bitcoin at $12,000 and receive it in December, or if he thinks the price might fall, he can buy an *option* to own one bitcoin at $12,000. He will need to pay a premium to own it, and the price of that premium goes up the longer he wants to keep the option.

In the same way that Thalus placed a deposit for the chance that the olive harvest would keep demand for the presses high, Manash will stand to reap considerable profit if Bitcoin rises in price.

Thalus would have given up his deposit if the demand for presses were low, so his losses would have been limited to the initial deposit he paid. In the same way, Manash's losses can never exceed the relatively small amount he paid for the option.

An options contract works like a hedge for peace of mind. You've fixed the price you'll buy the bitcoin at, so you win out if it's worth more later, and lose only your deposit if it isn't. If Bitcoin's price tumbles, you can buy it at that lower price instead.

So, if there's a buyer, who sells the option? Suppose Andika has bought some bitcoins a while back which are sitting in his wallet. He does not think Bitcoin is going up for the time being, so he sells some $12,000 calls and earns the premium on them. (Investors call this amount a *strike price*, or simply *strike*.) If the price of one bitcoin does rise higher than $12,000, he must still sell his bitcoins at this rate to fulfil the obligation of the option, so he is effectively betting against a dramatic price rise. Andika has sold a covered call option.

As another example, suppose Xiao is looking to get into Bitcoin, but is waiting for it to be priced lower, say at $10,000 per bitcoin, before buying. He can write and sell a put option with a strike of $10,000, and he will fulfil the obligation to buy at that rate if Bitcoin does plunge to this level. If it does not, then he will earn a premium from selling the option to another person. What is the catch? If Xiao is wrong and Bitcoin's value rises sharply, he *must* buy it at that higher rate to sell to the holder, losing any gains from the premiums.

This is just one way the options market has adapted to Bitcoin, and details would fill another book. There will be more types of actors like Manash, Andika and Xiao. But just like traditional finance, this is a fast-growing new market with many investment offices of all sizes looking for yield-enhancing structures.

Enter the IEO

One of the most famous scenes of Robert Bolt's play, *A Man for All Seasons*, has the 16th-century English statesman Thomas More dismissing a spy from his home. "Arrest him!" More's family urges, but More refuses.

His wife protests that the spy has broken God's laws. "Then let God arrest him," More answers. He is perfectly serious, because even someone as evil as the Devil has the right not to be arrested by human beings before he breaks a human law.

"So, you'd give the Devil the benefit of law!" his son-in-law, the lawyer William Roper, snaps.

"Yes! What would you do?" More retorts. "Cut a great road through the law to get after the Devil?"

"Yes! I'd cut down every law in England to do that!" declares Roper.

"Oh? And when the last law was down, and the Devil turned round on you, where would you hide, Roper, the laws all being flat?" More asks.

> This country is planted thick with laws, from coast to coast – man's laws, not God's. And if you cut them down – and you're just the man to do it – do you really think you could stand upright in the winds that would blow then? Yes, I'd give the Devil benefit of law, for my own safety's sake!

Bolt was using the character of Thomas More to warn against a drift towards lawlessness and anarchy, supposedly to better society, as by taking away the deterrent effect of the law, Roper's efforts would have the unintended consequence of taking away the protection of the innocent that came with it. More warned that it would end up creating a better place for the Devil, or at least human evil, to work unimpeded. A lawless system wouldn't be heaven, it would be hell!

This spirit sums up the state of token trading today. Eric Ervin, CEO of blockchain asset management firm Blockforce Capital, has said:[7] "In short, ICOs aren't dead, investors are just doing more due diligence and looking for more credible and vetted projects."

In the ICO's place are two new means of raising capital, the Initial Exchange Offering (IEO) and the Security Token Offering (STO). Both are ways by which investors are "given benefit of law", through the ability to buy tokens and therefore invest in blockchain projects in a safer, more vetted way. Where earlier, the ICO market represented a return to the Wild West, this is civilisation expanding and developing areas that were once lawless battlegrounds into orderly neighbourhoods. The result is more safety for everyone, even if the government has to impose regulations to create it.

ICOs were easy to participate in and receive bonuses from, with little red tape between investor and beneficiary. But the unregulated landscape (and the immutable nature of blockchains themselves) led to many of them being scams, or wasting large amounts of money on projects that realistically would never see the light of day. Investors received tokens, but as we've seen, this did not translate into part ownership of the company, something a conventional shareholder enjoys. If the price of the token drops and one can't trade it, it's worthless, like the currency of a failed country.

IEOs provide a layer of vetting by having the transfer of the company's coins hosted by a cryptocurrency exchange. As Steve Walters of *CoinBureau* wrote:[8] "IEOs are similar to the ICO, but the exchange takes full responsibility for the fundraising process, including vetting the blockchain project to determine if it is legitimate and likely to be successful."

In other words, the exchange acts as a middleman, adding a layer of assurance and regulation to the trade. The exchange also has a reputation to protect and must comply with its local regulations, and so would presumably have done the necessary homework. (Of course, this doesn't replace the fundamentals of due diligence and never investing more than you can lose.) However, this raises the bar for entry, and it can be expensive for a startup still in its early stages. That said, this method has enjoyed considerable success, as in the first half of 2019, IEOs raised a combined $1.63 billion.

"IEOs will allow regulators to more easily monitor that KYC and anti-money laundering rules are being followed," explained communications coach Edward Iftody. "Again, blockchain purists might hate this but I firmly believe regulation is necessary if we expect the masses to adopt this technology."[9]

Note, however, that the tokens sold through IEOs aren't different products from what you get from an ICO. They don't amount to part ownership and don't have intrinsic value, and nothing guarantees their value will not be worse off in the future.

STOres of Value

STOs emerged in an attempt to combine the flexibility of ICOs with the security and regulation of traditional IPOs. In an STO, project teams still conduct fundraising as in an ICO, but the investment product is considered to be a financial instrument regulated by the country in which it is offered. This means it is far less likely to be a scam, and investors enjoy the same protection as buyers of any other securities product.

"Unlike utility tokens that mostly represent future access to an issuing company's service or product, STOs usually represent the underlying interest in either profit sharing, voting rights, interest in equity, dividends [or] other benefits that their investors can gain," noted Andrey Sergeenkov in *CoinGape*.[10] A security token, therefore, is sold with the expectation of profit and is so classed as a security, in the same way that a share would be in an IPO. In other words, when a security token is traded on an exchange, it is assumed to be backed up by an external asset, and can qualify its holder for equity and dividends.

Because STOs are much more restricted both for buyers and coins, this method is not as popular. The investor pool is limited to accredited buyers, who are necessarily of high net worth and constitute a much smaller pool of potential contributors. However, STOs do open the door for one of blockchain's most anticipated uses, the ownership of real-world assets through "digitisation" of their value. (I'll say more about this in the next chapter.)

This means ICOs are evolving, not dying out. No one wants to fall victim to a scam, so there's a built-in momentum towards having more accountability and transparency on both sides, especially when following Know Your Customer (KYC) rules. ICOs *had* to change if they wanted to retain the trust of their customers, and open themselves up to legal regulation and scrutiny. Far from putting lawyers out of business (as has been joked about in the past), they're giving the profession a good time!

A Game of Coins

The wheels are turning, and in my previous book, I wrote about the difficulties that blockchain companies have in working with banks. They've seen a turnaround, with banks entering the space in their own way. With Facebook's new Diem token, to be stabilised by pegging its value to existing currencies and financial instruments, crypto is seen as worthy of a second look. Diem is one of an emerging family of *stablecoins*, and backs up its value with the US dollar. (Plans to add the euro, yen, pound and Singapore dollar were drawn up, but ultimately scaled back due to regulatory issues.)[11] Stablecoins, it has been promised, are "backed by assets such as traditional money deposits, short-term government securities or gold. They have the potential to be less volatile and more of a mainstream asset than existing cryptocurrencies like bitcoin."[12]

Whatever form the investment products of the future take, the most important development has been a building of the marketplace "thick with laws, from top to bottom". With scammers being weeded out, the space is more promising than ever.

When Zuckerberg first announced Libra, his former Harvard classmates (and early Bitcoin pioneers), Tyler and Cameron Winklevoss, were said to be welcoming him "to the party". The twins were the co-founders of crypto exchange Gemini Trust Co, which was "one of the first companies to win regulatory approval from New York state to launch its own stablecoin, the Gemini dollar."[13]

Tyler Winklevoss expects Diem to be "very good for crypto and very good for Bitcoin":

> A company with the stature of Facebook talking about the word 'crypto' demystifies it, takes out some fear for some people – it might add other fear for different reasons, maybe privacy or whatnot – but the fact that a publicly traded company that's

a huge part of our economy actually is doing something really serious in crypto very much mainstreams it and I think it's a big win for our space.

Libra's White Paper revealed that while it will run on a blockchain, although with a key difference besides its backing as a stablecoin, it is more centralised than Bitcoin, running from the servers of the Libra Association's member companies. This is so that it can handle the thousands of transactions a second needed to be a true global medium of exchange. "The goal is to have Libra be capable of handling 1,000 transactions per second; Bitcoin can only process seven transactions per second, but Visa's payment network can support 24,000 a second," wrote Bernard Marr at *Forbes*.[14] It is hoped that with the support of mainstream companies like Facebook, crypto can take off in a way it could not when it was simply Satoshi Nakamoto and his partners ten short years ago.

That said, the fundamentals still haven't changed. I've written about ICO red flags, but the process is still the same: you guess what's going to be popular based on the decisions the business leaders are making, their transparency and their engagement with the community, and the realism of their promises. There's still lots of estimation involved as, after all, when social media was emerging, no one knew if Friendster, Facebook or MySpace would win out. Of course, those who guessed Facebook are now doing very well!

One true story of coming back strong after deflation is Polkadot, which aimed to seamlessly enable blockchains to write onto each other. Initially founded by Ethereum pioneer and founder Dr Gavin Wood, it underwent a drastic fall in value after a developer error destroyed many of the coins in circulation. It recovered and is lucky to be remaining on its current path; many others have pivoted away, or their founders have quit entirely.

This brings me to a principle of valuation beyond the ones I have listed in my earlier book: *Do the founders remain accountable to the community, and actively work to turn a bad situation around?* In other words, do they believe in the idea enough to keep working on it, or at least pivot to a more realistic model?

Dr Wood and his team have done exactly this, which is a big part of why their tokens have since gone back up many times over their initial value, and their backers have emerged wealthier for it.

Your New Blocks
- Cryptocurrencies are being accepted as underlying assets, leading to derivative products such as futures and options being sold on exchanges.
- Stablecoins like Libra (now Diem) are new experiments in stabilising the value of a cryptocurrency by backing it up with fiat money, thereby opening up the possibility of them being used as a medium of exchange.
- The fundamentals of which projects merit your selection remain the same, with one addition consideration: that founders remain accountable to the community.

Endnotes

1. "Long Island Iced Tea Corp. to Rebrand as 'Long Blockchain Corp.'", GlobeNewswire, 21 December 2017, at https://www.globenewswire.com/news-release/2017/12/21/1268978/0/en/Long-Island-Iced-Tea-Corp-to-Rebrand-as-Long-Blockchain-Corp.html.
2. Stephen O'Neal, "Textbook Case of Crypto Hype: How Iced Tea Company Went Blockchain and Failed Despite a 289 Percent Stock Rise", *CoinTelegraph*, 12 March 2019, at https://cointelegraph.com/news/textbook-case-of-crypto-hype-how-iced-tea-company-went-blockchain-and-failed-despite-a-289-percent-stock-rise.
3. Daniel Palmer, "FBI Suspects Insider Trading in Long Island Iced Tea Blockchain Pivot", *Coindesk*, 25 July 2019, at https://www.coindesk.com/fbi-suspects-insider-trading-around-long-island-iced-teas-blockchain-pivot.
4. Scott Adams, *Dilbert*, at https://dilbert.com/strip/2019-09-29.
5. His name is also spelled as "Thales", and he is primarily known as a mathematician. A French multinational electrical systems company is so named in his honour.
6. Joe Weisenthal, "The Story Of The First-Ever Options Trade In Recorded History", *Business Insider*, 4 March 2012, at https://www.businessinsider.com/the-story-of-the-first-ever-options-trade-in-recorded-history-2012-3?IR=T.
7. Charles Bovaird, "Is the ICO Market Truly Dead?" *Forbes*, 16 January 2019, at https://www.forbes.com/sites/cbovaird/2019/01/16/is-the-ico-market-truly-dead.
8. Steve Walters, "ICO vs. STO vs. IEO: Comprehensive Guide To Token Fundraising", *CoinBureau*, 10 July 2019, at https://www.coinbureau.com/education/ico-sto-ieo.
9. Edward Iftody, "What's the difference between Crowdfunding, ICO's, IEO's and STO's?" *Medium*, 18 June 2019, at https://medium.com/swlh/whats-the-difference-between-crowdfunding-ico-s-ieo-s-and-sto-s-d4059f6b24ed.
10. Andrey Sergeenkov, "STO vs IEO, What Is the Difference and When Startups Should Choose One", *CoinGape*, 8 May 2019, at https://coingape.com/sto-vs-ieo-difference.
11. Reuters, "Diem, Facebook's rebranded Libra crypto project, to launch US dollar-pegged digital currency", *South China Morning Post*, 13 May 2021, at https://www.scmp.com/tech/big-tech/article/3133277/diem-facebooks-rebranded-libra-crypto-project-launch-us-dollar-pegged.
12. "US dollar to be main currency backing Facebook's Libra, Singapore dollar also included: Der Spiegel", *The Business Times*, 21 September 2019, at https://www.businesstimes.com.sg/banking-finance/us-dollar-to-be-main-currency-backing-facebooks-libra-singapore-dollar-also-included.
13. Gemini, because they're twins. Get it? Quoted in Vildana Hajric and Alastair Marsh, "Winklevoss Twins' Message to Zuckerberg: 'Welcome to the Party'", *Bloomberg*, 11 July 2019, at https://www.bloomberg.com/news/articles/2019-07-10/winklevoss-twins-message-to-zuckerberg-welcome-to-the-party.
14. Bernard Marr, "Facebook's Blockchain-Based Cryptocurrency Libra: Everything You Need To Know", *Forbes*, 7 October 2019, at https://www.forbes.com/sites/bernardmarr/2019/10/07/facebooks-blockchain-based-cryptocurrency-libra-everything-you-need-to-know.

Chapter 4

FROM CURRENCY TO TOKEN

> You must be shapeless, formless, like water. When you pour water in a cup, it becomes the cup. When you pour water in a bottle, it becomes the bottle. When you pour water in a teapot, it becomes the teapot. Water can drip and it can crash. Become like water, my friend.
> **Bruce Lee**

What You'll Learn
- Some thoughts on the future of blockchain and P2P businesses.
- The concerns behind Bitcoin's use as a backup for fiat money.
- How practically anything can be tokenised, and the way it shapes business in the future.

Are there precedents of how crypto will transform the Web's future, and usher in what Polkadot calls Web3? The best one I can think of emerged in the Internet's transformation into the largest multimedia distribution tool the world had ever seen, back in the days of music CDs and dial-up networking. The software that would enable peer-to-peer file sharing across a decentralised network was still in its infancy in 1999, but ideas began to be bounced back and forth between computer hackers on messaging service Internet Relay Chat (IRC).

A teenager in Massachusetts named Shawn Fanning would hang out there, and one spring day, he told the group about his new project: a program that would allow users to quickly and easily swap music files. (His nickname on the group was "Napster", from a "trash talker making fun of his hair on the basketball court."[1])

Then, as now, everyone wanted the latest music, but very few wanted to pay for it. It was a difficult process downloading it from the Internet, but Fanning had a dream of making the process easier. The group liked his idea, and others began showing interest in helping him. Eventually, Shawn's uncle, John, incorporated the company, attracting investors to the new Napster Inc.

The group grew quickly, attracting venture capital, software engineers and lawyers. Early team members feared that the work might be illegal, but investor Yosi Amram had "done some legal work and had a legal opinion", according to fellow investor Eileen Richardson. It was felt that if Shawn Fanning's work ended up changing how music was distributed for the better, Richardson went on, "any issues would solve themselves."[2]

Napster's growth was rapid and by 2001, its user base had peaked at 26.4 million worldwide. Alex Winter wrote in *Wired*:[3]

> This was still the dialup era, and even though the web had taken us out of the text-only dark

ages, trying to find online communities or share music meant navigating a morass of impenetrable newsgroups or unreliable MP3 sites. Napster connected us easily to people around the world, turning others onto our music at incredible speed.

But the record industry moved to protect itself, and Napster found itself in the very legal trouble it had feared. By leaking music ahead of official release, record labels alleged that it was aiding piracy, violating copyright and depriving artistes of revenue. While a significant number of users felt that file sharing on Napster was actually spreading music by word of mouth and promoting it, the record labels won the day in court. Napster appealed the verdict to a higher court but lost. In late 2001, the network was completely shut down. It would be the first legal case against a P2P network, and one of the earliest uses of the disruptive power of the Internet.

Of the online businesses that came into being during the dot-com era, Napster is one of the few whose name continues to this day, although in a different, more centralised model from what Fanning had envisioned. Today, various companies, including Napster's modern incarnation, operate paid music streaming services, but Fanning was the pioneer who showed how it could be done.

The fate of Napster and similar services laid bare how much power large companies and governments had to maintain the status quo. Just before his announcement of Bitcoin, Satoshi Nakamoto pointed out that while Napster had a decentralised P2P structure, it was still a registered company with offices, leadership and paperwork. That was what enabled its record industry foes to have it decapitated. This very vulnerability inspired Nakamoto to build Bitcoin (and its underlying blockchain technology) as pure P2P systems with no central authority to shut down.[4]

The growth of Bitcoin as a financial product has led to an entire ecosystem of alternative cryptocurrencies, with varying amounts of availability, block generation and transaction time, and centralisation. One might try to reduce the wait time for miners to authorise transactions, another might give developers more "power" to reverse fraudulent ones and so protect customers, or yet a third might do more to hide user identities and preserve anonymity.

One of the most promising is the decentralised application framework known as Ethereum, which uses its own crypto (called "ether") and allows automated transfer of tokens and materials over its own blockchain. The processes that govern these transactions are called "smart contracts". As Ethereum is still trustless, the smart contracts are programmed to only trigger transactions when certain pre-programmed conditions are met. There is, effectively, no more wiggle room to back out, nor any need for an escrow account to temporarily hold the funds – and, of course, no danger of the recipient disappearing with my ether without giving me what I paid for!

The debate over Bitcoin will continue for many years, and concerns have grown over how decentralised and immune to government interference it really is. That hasn't stopped it from becoming a "backup" currency to store value, especially in uncertain times. After all, governments and businesses still falter economically, taking billions of dollars of value with them. Banning Bitcoin is not certain to go well with their own citizens.

Add that to the fact that the Bitcoin network will need so much computing power to tamper with it that it may not be worth the effort in the first place.[5]

If anything, more recent government actions have made the case for a reserve currency more relevant than ever. In February 2019, Spain's BBVA (the country's second largest bank) froze thousands of Chinese nationals' accounts completely without warning, in a supposed attempt to stop money-laundering from China under Spanish law. Despite the assurances, and whether it was a legal move or not, it remained the case that thousands of people were suddenly restricted from accessing their money overnight. "This is a frightening reminder that banks have the power to immediately block access to people's money without any warning," warned Ian Karamanov in *CoinStaker*.[6] "On a larger scale when more banks are involved, this scenario will make the great depression look like child's play."

People who live in troubled economies have long known of banks' ability (and sometimes willingness) to confiscate vast amounts of wealth without warning. Even in the United States, the "land of the free", there are reports that the Internal Revenue Service:[7]

> … has seized millions of dollars in cash from individuals and businesses that obtained the money legally …

> The IRS pursued hundreds of cases from 2012 to 2015 on suspicion of structuring, but with no indications of connections to any criminal activity. Simply depositing cash in sums of less than $10,000 was all that it took to arouse agents' suspicions, leading to the eventual seizure and forfeiture of millions of dollars in cash from people not otherwise suspected of criminal activity.

Notice that the rules the IRS used were set up to combat drug trafficking and terrorism, using tax structuring as a "trigger" for further investigation. In fact, the news release indicated that following encouragement to quickly open and close cases by the Justice Department, the IRS deliberately targeted businesses "that had obtained their money legally", so that they could quickly resolve cases through negotiation, rather than engage in the lengthy, complicated effort of pursuing criminal cases. In a sense, a government agency that abuses its powers is worse than a politician doing so, because the politician can be voted out; but where do you go to vote out the agency?

If anything, it's a warning to be careful what you incentivise. But for now, let it serve as a reminder that fiat money is not the stable, secure value store that many people think it is. Governments are no more immune to greed, incompetence and other human failings than any other organisation.

Tokenising the World

In September 2018, the first tokenised painting was sold – not to an individual purchaser, but hundreds of bidders each owning a "share" of Andy Warhol's painting, 14 Small Electric Chairs. The auction was conducted by Singapore-based blockchain art investment platform Maecenas. Mark Emem of CCN wrote:[8] "Approximately US$1.7 million was raised in the cryptocurrency auction for a 31.5% stake of the artwork whose total valuation was US$5.6 million. More than 800 bidders signed up for the auction which was conducted entirely using a smart contract."

At the auction, bidders could pay for a share of the painting in Bitcoin, Ethereum or Maecenas' own ART cryptocurrencies. By breaking ownership of a multimillion-dollar asset into chunks, Maecenas was doing for a piece of art what was once only available for entire companies.

Where blockchain shines is its ability to break down ownership of practically anything into chunks. This applies even to things that don't lend themselves to division, be it real estate, art pieces or even farm animals. After all, you can't cut someone's milk cow into pieces for others to own, or deface a valuable painting! (Mr Bean got away with doing it to Whistler's Mother in his 1997 movie, but the rest of us aren't so lucky.)

This process, presently being pursued by hundreds of startups around the world, is called tokenisation. In fact, Bitcoin itself can be said to be a tokenisation of electricity and computing power, given that these are the resources you "pay" to win the Bitcoin mining race.

Put simply, tokenisation is the expression of shared ownership through digital representation of an item. Its ownership is represented as a digital token or "coin" that can be generated, publicly traded, bought and sold on a blockchain, so there is no doubt as to whom it belongs. It looks a lot like the stock or Forex market, doesn't it?

At crypto news site *Blockonomi*, Oliver Dale divided tokenisation and ownership into three broad categories: intangibles, non-fungible goods and fungible goods.[9]

An intangible is merely an idea, a concept that has no physical presence. Yet, they're enormously powerful and direct the way we do business. "Copyrights, patents, brand recognition, and goodwill are prime examples," wrote Dale.

> These concepts, however, can be represented by a token or many tokens on a blockchain system. They can be assigned a unique identifier and then traded, gaining their value from the market. Creating tokens for intangible assets gives them a solid backing for transfer and a secure guarantee of their legitimacy.

Blockchain enables this to be done in a secure, fully transparent way that avoids much of the legal paperwork required otherwise. There is no way to fudge or bail out of a smart contract – that is, an automated computer script will send tokenised payments if (and only if) certain agreed-upon conditions are met. The result will be instantly verifiable and visible to everyone.

A second category would be fungible, or mutually interchangeable, goods. Think of water, oil, rice or even gold – a litre of water is equivalent to another litre of water, a barrel of one type of oil is tradeable at the same price for another barrel of the same type of oil and a one-kilogram sack of rice is worth the same as another.

Dale pointed out that: "Very often, fungible assets are backed by a physical resource, somewhere – gold or wheat in a warehouse, water or oil in a pipeline."[10]

> Fungible assets are often dealt with in bulk form, and delivery simply cannot be done instantaneously. A shipment of 10,000 short tons of line pipe, for instance, is pretty bulky. Transferring ownership of that asset from one entity to another either involves moving 10,000 short tons of steel or creating a paper trail, whereby the steel is transferred via a trusted third party, like a bank, to the new owner before it physically moves.

What tokenising the asset (like so much steel) does is create a digital *representation* of that asset on a blockchain, and make the transfer using a smart contract. Rather than recording everything down by hand, all the relevant information that pertains to storing and shipping the steel is instantly transferred, saving time and manpower.

But what makes blockchains so powerful is their ability to trade tokenised representations of non-fungible goods, like the Warhol painting. We're effectively creating digital "shares" that can be traded and broken down into smaller units that bear the same tamper-proof sign of authenticity, and those units can be sold to anyone.

Besides the art world, one promising field that tokenisation is disrupting is real estate. Suppose I owned an apartment in the Marina Bay area and wanted to partially sell it to tenants, both to generate income and increase their sense of ownership of the place. However, my tenants can't own just five or six square metres of the place, I can't sell just part of the physical place to them. The apartment itself, like 14 Small Electric Chairs before 2018, must be bought or sold as a single unit.

But if several companies working in the blockchain real estate space develop their products of fractional property sale further, I'd be able to do exactly that. A digital token representing the apartment could be set up in my cryptocurrency "wallet", and I could choose to sell part of it to you, and another part to someone else. As a part owner, the property is available for you to rent any time it's available – you only need to pay the rent for the portion you don't already own. For instance, if you hold 25 per cent ownership, you only pay rent for the remaining 75 per cent. The distributed ownership means more people care for the place, and your share can be retained as a value store (useful for when the land value increases) or sold to another buyer.

This opens up great possibilities for new investments into the developing world. You could partner with farmers by investing in, and thereby part-owning, their flocks or fields. You could help small businesses in a more secure way than the traditional approach of micro-loans; or teachers or aid workers through tokenisation of their schools and supplies. In 2017, the United Nations' World Food Programme began testing a blockchain-based approach to improving transaction security and identity management. During a mission to provide humanitarian aid to Pakistan's Sindh Province:[11]

> An internet-connected smartphone authenticated and recorded payments from the U.N. agency to food vendors, ensuring the recipients got help, the merchants got paid and the agency didn't lose track of its money.

Tokenisation has made possible a new way of thinking about securities and financial products. Today, a startup can simply launch an IEO or STO, and sell something very similar to shares of itself to the public.

Bitcoin and other cryptocurrencies are effectively an "opt-out" option from national economies, but in a way, they are still like the Wild West. As the cases of crypto stores being hacked showed, the kinks are still being worked out. But in time to come, they'll be a powerful new tool to get things done, take ownership of new assets, or (God forbid) survive in the wake of economic collapse.

Where Crypto Derives its Value

Bitcoin, and other cryptocurrencies like Ether and Ripple, get their value because of some use they have that makes them desirable. They are both a medium of exchange and a store of value, and the value of the latter depends on how useful it is for the former. As John P Kelleher explained in his *Investopedia* article: "... if bitcoin does not achieve success as a medium of exchange, it will have no practical utility and thus no intrinsic value and won't be appealing as a store of value."[12]

Notice that cryptocurrencies' main selling points have emphasised how useful they are as mediums of exchange. For instance, the Ethereum network's "smart contract" system is a way of automating payments and, by extension, the transfer of value from one user to another, in a specific way that does not require the involved parties to trust each other, and only when certain conditions are met.

Besides mining it yourself, there are two ways you can obtain crypto. You can be paid in it for a good or service in place of cash, or you can buy it on an *exchange*. In the same way that a stock exchange is a place where you buy and sell part ownership of various companies, a cryptocurrency exchange is an online hub where you do the same for different kinds of crypto. You can buy them with fiat money, or exchange one crypto for another.

Now it is true, as many legacy investors have pointed out, that cryptocurrencies are just computer files with no inherent value. "You're just paying for thin air," scoff many.

But then again, how much more inherent value does a computer file have than a piece of paper, or a stamped piece of metal? Fiat money may be backed up by government institutions, but it will have value only as long as those institutions avoid the problems that have plagued authorities from the beginning – revolution, economic collapse, corruption and many more.

In Forex, we analyse currencies to determine their value and how much we're willing to pay for them, and cryptocurrencies pass the tests that every financial product must in order to be worth what they are.

For instance:

1. *Is it fungible?* In other words, can one unit be interchangeable with another? We treat a tattered, stained $100 note as having the same value as a pristine, unused one straight from the bank. In the same way, one bitcoin is worth exactly as much as another bitcoin.
2. *Is it a scarce resource?* "For something to be considered a currency, there needs to be a limited supply of it ... For example, there is a finite amount of gold in the world, which gives it a value as a currency," pointed out Matthew Howells-Barby in his article on *The Coin Offering*.[13] "Similarly, only 21 million bitcoins will ever be released, which gives Bitcoin its value."

   Other cryptocurrencies have different limits, but their value derives from there only being a finite amount. This creates an incentive either to hold on to it, in hopes that it will appreciate in value, or spend it on something worth more to you.
3. *Can ownership be easily transferred from one party to another?* This is how it gains any ability to be used in trading for goods and services. Bitcoin (and most other cryptos) enables this for anyone with an Internet connection, and it happens with far fewer checks and verifications than a fiat transfer.

   This is not to say that Bitcoin and other cryptos are perfect. Because miners must authorise the transactions

– and only the winning miner of the ten-minute race can do this – it is customary to add a transaction fee to incentivise the miner to include your transaction in the authorised block. Because winning the race is time and energy-consuming, miners have an incentive to include those transactions that pay them better. Bitcoin limits block sizes to 1 MB in total, meaning that only so many transactions can be accommodated.

Harsh Agrawal at *CoinSutra* puts this number at 4,194 to 4,559. He continues: [14]

So as a result of free-market users deciding the fees of the transaction, as well as the limited 1 MB space, finding a place in the blocks has become expensive.

Free market users who can't wait for longer durations for their transactions to be confirmed naturally attach more fee per bytes to their transactions, thereby pushing the free market average fees higher.

Higher transaction fees increase the chance that your transaction will have a place in the next few blocks to be mined, a waiting time of around ten to 30 minutes.

In other words, if you're not willing to pay more, Bitcoin transactions between buyer and seller can take much longer than simply handing over the amount in fiat. But cryptocurrencies are always evolving, and the problem

of long transaction times may have been resolved (or at least mitigated) by the time you read this.
4   *Is it divisible into smaller units?* In the same way that dollars and cents can be traded, Bitcoin can also be exchanged in smaller amounts than the thousands of dollars a single bitcoin fetches today. Sophie Bearman pointed out in her CNBC article that it is, in fact, "... trivially divisible, meaning you can buy a small item like a doughnut with it as easily as you can buy a house or even a mansion."[15]

The smallest divisible unit of a bitcoin is the satoshi (one ten-millionth of a bitcoin), named in honour of its creator.

As cryptocurrencies are still in their infancy (Bitcoin itself is just over a decade old as I write this), much remains to be found out about their use, value and interaction with government regulations. Much of their volatility comes from this: when China banned all cryptocurrency trading in late 2017, out of fear that many ICOs were scamming investors of their money, Bitcoin prices fell by hundreds of dollars; but when they were regulated and re-introduced, their value increased to more than it had been before the ban.

Other countries have taken different approaches, depending on the number and veracity of the ICOs there. In Singapore, there remains a dialogue between its central bank (the Monetary Authority of Singapore or MAS) and various crypto startups and banks. The government's attitude is one of careful, stepwise experimentation; its research indicates that blockchain consortia and projects are about to be embarked on over these few years. Project Ubin is one such attempt to create a proof-of-concept aimed at facilitating inter-bank payments on blockchain, using a tokenised form of the Singapore dollar.[16]

Governments and banks are approaching the decentralised nature of cryptos very carefully – they don't have the legacy protections in place for other financial products, nor do they have decision-makers who can be held accountable in the event of a crash or market failure.

If, for instance, the Bitcoin network went completely offline tomorrow, billions of dollars in value would be lost forever, unless a working copy of one or more ledgers could be retrieved and "rolled back". And no one – not you, not me, not Satoshi Nakamoto, not miners – could be held responsible in any way.

Precisely because crypto is so new, and its transactions irreversible, many painful lessons have had to be learnt. It is in these cases that the governing authorities have to identify how people can be protected.

In the world of aviation, there's a saying that regulations are written in blood. In other words, they come from painful experiences that have inconvenienced, injured or killed thousands of people.

In that spirit, I must urge caution when entering the crypto space. In the same way that lives have been lost in aviation disasters, fortunes and entire savings accounts have been wiped out in crypto mishaps.

At the end of 2018, QuadrigaCX was one of the largest crypto exchanges to operate in Canada. But all of that changed when founder and CEO Gerald Cotten suddenly died while volunteering at an orphanage in India. It turned out access to millions of dollars' worth of cryptocurrency assets (belonging to customers) were stored on encrypted devices, and as his laptop and smartphone were locked, he had taken their money to the grave with him. As I write, customers are trying to recover the money they lost, and it will be some time before a painful (but preventable) legal affair comes to an end.

But if something so novel can depend on just one man's life or death, it's a clear sign that the industry has more growing to do.

Yet the genie is out of the bottle, and that growth is happening right before our eyes. The long and short of it all? We'll let the respected crypto pioneer Anthony Pompliano of Morgan Creek Digital close this chapter: "The legacy financial institutions are doing more to help the adoption of Bitcoin than they realize. Long Bitcoin, Short the Bankers!"[17]

Your New Blocks
- The traditional role of Bitcoin and other cryptocurrencies, one of medium of exchange and value store, is evolving as governments get involved. Note that the authorities' role is to safely regulate the industry, but they will not do this perfectly and it is up to startups and financial institutions to advise them.
- Perhaps blockchains' biggest strength is the ability to digitise ownership of real assets – consider this when picking which projects to back.
- Caution is needed when entering and trading in the crypto space. Many of the rules needed to protect investors and users have yet to be written, and the risk remains high even if measures are being instituted to mitigate it.

Endnotes

1. Richard Nieva, "Ashes to ashes, peer to peer: An oral history of Napster," *Fortune*, 5 September 2013, at https://fortune.com/2013/09/05/ashes-to-ashes-peer-to-peer-an-oral-history-of-napster.
2. Alex Winter, "The Short History of Napster 1.0", *Wired*, 16 April 2013, at https://www.wired.com/2013/04/napster.
3. Alex Winter, "The Short History of Napster 1.0", *Wired*, 16 April 2013, at https://www.wired.com/2013/04/napster.
4. Satoshi Nakamoto, "Re: Bitcoin P2P e-cash paper," Cryptography Mailing List, 7 November 2008, at bit.ly/1truasJ.
5. It is, however, not impossible. For more, see: Gideon Greenspan, "The Blockchain Immutability Myth", *CoinDesk*, 9 May 2017, at https://www.coindesk.com/blockchain-immutability-myth.
6. Ian Karamanov, "BBVA Freeze 5000 Chinese Clients Accounts Without Warning", *CoinStaker*, 20 February 2019, at https://www.coinstaker.com/bbva-chinese-clients-accounts-warning.
7. Christopher Ingraham, "The IRS took millions from innocent people because of how they managed their bank accounts, inspector general finds", *The Washington Post*, 5 April 2017, at https://www.washingtonpost.com/news/wonk/wp/2017/04/05/the-irs-took-millions-from-innocent-people-because-of-how-they-managed-their-bank-accounts-inspector-general-finds/?utm_term=.543a1903bd9e.
8. Mark Emem, "Andy Warhol's Multi-Million Dollar Painting Tokenized and Sold on Blockchain", *Yahoo! Finance*, 6 September 2018, at https://finance.yahoo.com/news/andy-warhol-multi-million-dollar-162928721.html.
9. Oliver Dale, "Democratizing Ownership & Real-World Assets on the Blockchain", *Blockonomi*, 31 July 2018, at https://blockonomi.com/tokenization-blockchain.
10. Oliver Dale, "Democratizing Ownership & Real-World Assets on the Blockchain", *Blockonomi*, 31 July 2018, at https://blockonomi.com/tokenization-blockchain.
11. Nir Kshetri, "Could Blockchain Technology Help The World's Poorest?" *General Electric*, 11 July 2017, at https://www.ge.com/news/reports/blockchain-technology-help-worlds-poorest.
12. John P. Kelleher, "Why Do Bitcoins Have Value?" *Investopedia*, 14 February 2019, at https://www.investopedia.com/ask/answers/100314/why-do-bitcoins-have-value.asp.
13. Matthew Howells-Barby, "How Do Cryptocurrencies Have Value?" *The Coin Offering*, 5 March 2018, at https://thecoinoffering.com/learn/how-do-cryptocurrencies-have-value.
14. Harsh Agrawal, "How Much Bitcoin Transaction Fees To Pay For Confirmed Transaction?" *CoinSutra*, 13 October 2018, at https://coinsutra.com/bitcoin-transaction-fees/#How_Is_Bitcoin_Transaction_Fee_Decided.
15. Sophie Bearman, "As bitcoin's price plunges, skeptics say the cryptocurrency has no value. Here's one argument for why they're wrong," CNBC, 16 January 2018, at https://www.cnbc.com/2018/01/16/skeptics-say-bitcoin-has-no-value-heres-why-theyre-wrong.html
16. For more, see: Deloitte and MAS, "The future is here – Project Ubin: SGD on Distributed Ledger", Monetary Authority of Singapore, 2017, at https://www.mas.gov.sg/-/media/MAS/ProjectUbin/Project-Ubin--SGD-on-Distributed-Ledger.pdf.
17. Shilpa Lama, "Bitcoin Is Fast Evolving Into a Global Reserve Currency, Says Morgan Creek Digital Founder", *Blokt*, 19 February 2019, at https://blokt.com/news/bitcoin-is-fast-evolving-into-a-global-reserve-currency-says-morgan-creek-digital-founder.

Chapter 5

EMERGING FROM CRYPTO WINTER

> What profit has he who works in that in which he labors? I have seen the burden which God has given to the sons of men to be afflicted with. He has made everything beautiful in its time. He has also set eternity in their hearts, yet so that man can't find out the work that God has done from the beginning even to the end. I know that there is nothing better for them than to rejoice, and to do good as long as they live. Also that every man should eat and drink, and enjoy good in all his labor, is the gift of God.
> Ecclesiastes 3:9–13 (World English Bible)

What You'll Learn
- Why recent developments were called a "crypto winter" and brighter days are ahead.
- There is a basis for confidence in the future, as any untested new technology has teething pains over many years.
- How I handled my own failures as a trader and bounced back.

If I were asked to sum up what has changed after the dreaded "crypto winter" and the emergence of (for now) clearer winners and losers, I'd make the following observations.

First, the fundamentals haven't changed a bit. Bitcoin's protocol is as solid as the day it was created. Only what has been built on top of it that allow us to interact with it more easily has developed, in the same way the structure, foundation and utility systems in the same building don't change in spite of the different uses it will be put to over the years.

Of course, blockchain's basic protocols have been adjusted many times over the years, to compensate for weaknesses and fit into the ecosystem of businesses and their individual needs. No blockchain will ever be everything to everyone, and it's up to you to decide which projects to back, which to merely watch and which to discount altogether.

One of Bitcoin's major drawbacks, the long wait before a transaction can be confirmed, is being addressed through various protocols and altcoins, and as these efforts grow more successful, it's hoped that it will be less volatile in the future. It does, however, remain one of the best investments you can make as I write.

Second, circumstances don't remain static. COVID-19 is a case in point, and entire industries were forced to change or die, and governments enacted harsh, drastic measures in response to it. Part of the reason for Bitcoin's new-found popularity seems to be a reaction to the vast, sweeping new powers politicians used (and are still using) to lock down entire countries, put tight controls on what people could do, and print money and thereby drive down its value. People wanted an alternative value store that politicians couldn't touch, a role Bitcoin and other cryptos were designed to fill in the first place.

Third, because cryptocurrencies are entirely your own property, and COVID-19 lockdowns have shown them to have a concrete use, the debate over them has instead become less polarised and more accepting that they'll be a part of the financial ecosystem going forward. Guggenheim Investments, one of the largest investment funds in the world, announced in late 2020 that ten per cent of its portfolio will include alternative instruments like Bitcoin, and it's difficult to get a larger backer than that!

"We made the decision to start allocating towards bitcoin when bitcoin was at $10,000. It's a little more challenging with the current price of $20,000. It's amazing over a short period of time how big of a run we had," Guggenheim Chief Investment Officer Scott Minerd told Bloomberg Markets. "Having said that, our fundamental work shows that bitcoin should be worth about $400,000." Minerd added, "Bitcoin actually has a lot of the attributes of gold and at the same time has an unusual value in terms of transaction."[1]

Confidence in it is such that even payment services like PayPal and Square are allowing it to be used in transactions, and bought and sold on their platforms by American users. Because there'll only ever be a finite amount, its value can't help but go up.

Transaction fees are also coming down, and when you move large financial products around, you will definitely pay a comparable sum in transfer fees. It's still cheaper than the traditional method, and the entire market remains under as much government scrutiny as possible.

As I write, those investments I've made within my local sphere are doing relatively well, such as Kyber and Zilliqa. Another investment I named in my previous book was Polkadot, which has also made a strong comeback from a disastrous error that wiped out a large portion of its coins. This reinforces my belief that the "crypto winter" was one of any number of Darwinian filter events during a time of testing that revealed which projects were really plausible and which were just wishful thinking.

There's room for optimism, and if you've been burned, I urge you not to give up on the market altogether. Hedge fund founder Ray Dalio noted in his book, *Principles: Life and Work*:[2]

> "He who lives by the crystal ball is destined to eat ground glass" is a saying I quoted a lot in those days. Between 1979 and 1982, I had eaten enough glass to realize that what was most important wasn't knowing the future – it was knowing how to react appropriately to the information available at each point in time.

When Dalio took any position in the markets, he would write down why, and the criteria he had used to do so. Over time, he refined that criteria into a system he could use to decide what would perform well, over and over again. Your own trading patterns, and those of your mentors, very probably hold the information you need to evaluate any crypto project on its own merits, provided, of course, you allocate your funds wisely. Never trade with your budget for daily living!

Keeping Your Head

By April 2020, the COVID-19 pandemic had led to thousands of infections around Singapore. The government issued the Orange Alert and a lockdown of the country it called the Circuit Breaker. This measure closed public areas and forced businesses to institute as much working from home as possible, and was to last until June, after which gradual reopening would take place.

My employer decided to split its team across two workplaces. One group would remain in the main headquarters at the Marina Bay Financial Centre, while the other worked out of Changi Business Park in the eastern part of the island.

I led the Changi team during this period, and felt a little like Noah on the Ark. He could look out of the window and see the floodwaters, as could I – a stone's throw away stood Singapore's single largest COVID-19 treatment facility, a massive convention hall at the Expo transformed into a dedicated infectious diseases hospital for the thousands of foreign workers who had been infected by the virus.

The risk of infection was considered so high that everyone who did not absolutely need to come to the office worked from home, and those who had to be at the office were required to be religious in disinfecting and staying clean. I sanitised my hands so much I nearly suffered chemical burns! Fortunately, the virus has been well-contained as I write months later, and the treatment facility has since been returned to its original use.

I've had plenty of time to reflect on how difficult situations need to be handled, as over the recent years from 2013 onward, it has felt like we have gone from the frying pan into the fire. My rough and unusual childhood, ironically enough, has helped me to keep my head when more sheltered traders might have given in to despair. Handled the right way, difficult experiences in childhood do contribute towards building resilience for the future. Mine are no exception – my earliest memory is literally of being kidnapped by my father from my mother's home! He barged in with several of his friends and grabbed me from the bathtub, pulling me right out of her hands. (He wound up returning me about a week later, after taking care of me proved too much for him.)

I grew up in one of Kuala Lumpur's roughest neighbourhoods, and quickly learnt to watch out for and anticipate trouble, reading warning signs that less seasoned people missed and leaving before a fight broke out. This was only possible when you were calm under pressure and in anticipation of threats, rather than being just left to react when trouble started. I grew so used to operating in that mental place the US Marines call "left of bang" that it's now my default state of mind.[3]

That's not to say a rough upbringing is necessarily better. My life could have turned out very differently; perhaps I was also lucky to have met the right teachers and mixed with the right friends. I was able to study and got into a good school. My family sacrificed much to give me a chance at securing a scholarship, and I was successful enough to be able to go overseas to study before finding work in a bank.

My upbringing did enable me to withstand the pressure of making money for the bank, with so many things being beyond my control. Self-defence experts warn that in a fight, things can spiral out of control very easily – you can make every mistake in the book and still come out unscathed thanks to blind luck, and you can just as easily do everything right and still get killed.

It's the same in the markets, but paradoxically, the first thing one should do when something goes wrong is to own the mistake and not blame anyone else. Failure is a part of the process; think of it as finding a new piece of the jigsaw puzzle you must put together. "Every problem you find is an opportunity to improve your machine," Dalio says. "Identifying and not tolerating problems is one of the most important and disliked things people can do."

It's fine to celebrate success, but it's also important to do so when you've learned what's gone wrong. There's nothing wrong with mistakes, and they are often how we learn where we and others are falling short. What should not be tolerated in ourselves and our teams is a failure to learn from mistakes. "I don't want to suggest that it's all luck or it's all accidental, but you have to get yourself into harm's way," Bill Winters, CEO of Standard Chartered, told me in a discussion in July 2020. "And then when the harm comes at you, you've got to be able to separate what might actually be beneficial from what really is harmful and needs to be avoided."

Too often, we overemphasise perfection and getting things right the first time, and are conditioned to see failure as a sign of weakness rather than the opportunity for improvement that it is. If we harshly punish mistakes, we encourage people to hide them instead of correcting them.

That's a terrible mistake in itself, because we run the risk of building what Dalio calls "a culture that would not only be dishonest but crippled in its ability to learn and grow." People, especially leaders, must be open to learning from mistakes, not prevented from making them in the first place.

As Bill put it to me during our discussion:

> I like to be in positions where I'm uncomfortable because I must try to learn the ropes. I don't like failing or making mistakes, but I do acknowledge them, review my situation regularly to understand when they happen, and then learn from them.
> I always put myself in a position of being approachable, so I can learn something from my team.

That hit home especially for me when I joined Tudor, after four successful years at Goldman Sachs. It was especially significant for Tudor, as I was its first hire from a market-maker position at a bank. In 2013, I started strong and made over $100 million in returns, out of a $500 million fund. I became one of its top-performing managers; my assets under management multiplied in value, and I was appointed CEO of Tudor's Singapore office.

Sadly, that did not last. In July, I went into a losing streak, and several times the losses were so bad I had to take a time-out from trading. I remember that Singapore was hit hard by the infamous haze from the forest fires in Indonesia then, and my wife asked me to take a break overseas with the kids. I refused and stubbornly tried to win back my losses, only to lose even more.

My mental health suffered, and so did my family life. My firm also gave me a lot of heat, and I was repeatedly asked why I hadn't been more careful. I was getting what Bill calls development feedback, or discussions on how I could be more effective. One of Bill's words of advice has since reminded me of that period:

> If you're repeating the same thing and getting the same results, you're not making any progress. You can try to find the reasons why, but if it's the nature of the way that you behave; a style or sensibility you're unable to address; or a quality we're supposed to get but are unable to acquire, it's really not working.

Over 2014, I had several hard conversations with my boss, Paul Tudor Jones. "Why can't I make money anymore?" I asked him. He worked with me to fine-tune my trading analysis and execution, and while I'd like to say there was an immediate turnaround, it took too long to get my winning ways back. I did stem the bleeding, losing less but still paying the price in bid offer spreads.

Put simply, what I gained was barely enough to cover the costs of trading, making my net contribution in the low positives. I was gaining money for the firm only a little bit faster than I was losing it, and by 2016, Paul decided it was time to stop investing in Singapore for the time being. I got the axe that June, a few months before he exited Singapore entirely.[4] It was painful, but we both knew that was the best decision for the wider company.

I was badly depressed, though I'm thankful that my family held together and I could still support them. That was when I decided to delve into the startup scene, using my knowledge to help entrepreneurs find office space and partners, build strong business models and secure capital from the right places. When it came time to return to traditional banking, I joined a new bank with a humble heart and clear mind. That experience got me trading much better than I could ever have done just a few years before.

My advice: if you're emerging from bad decisions like the ones I made, the first thing is to keep your head. Detach if you can from the bad trade, and try to take the perspective of an outsider examining a stranger's decisions. Getting good advice helps, and on hindsight, I wish I had taken steps to mitigate the distance my job title was creating between my colleagues and I. People were hesitant to examine my trades and add their two cents' worth, and as a result I operated with far less restraint, accountability and insight than I ever had in my life.

As we'll see in the Conclusion to this book, the late Tony Hsieh's downfall and descent into bizarre behaviour isn't the anomaly many of us think it is – it can happen to anyone.

When you're able to stabilise the situation, consider entering a new field that's related to the previous one. I found mine in blockchain startups willing to hear from an educated but untested blockchain novice like me, and allowed me to share with them what I had learnt from traditional business. We guided each other into what I still believe is the future of banking and finance, and I'll always be grateful for that.

Your New Blocks
- There's room for optimism, with the strong possibility of improved, more secure blockchain-based and derived financial products. Confidence in them is rising again, even if many promised uses are still some years away.
- Resilience is important, especially when things don't go your way and it's a bad situation all around. Cultivate resilience in any way you can.
- Sometimes, detachment is needed to make better decisions, as is accountability to others and the ability to freely discuss mistakes and faults.
- A change in setting and the nature of your work could be the shot you need to do better.

Endnotes)
1 Kevin Helms, "Guggenheim Investments: Bitcoin Is Worth $400,000 Based on Scarcity, Relative Valuation to Gold", *Bitcoin.com*, 18 December 2020, at https://news.bitcoin.com/guggenheim-investments-bitcoin-worth-400000-scarcity-relative-valuation-to-gold.
2 Ray Dalio, *Principles: Life and Work* (New York: Simon and Schuster, 2017).
3 Patrick Van Horne and Jason A Riley, *Left of Bang: How the Marine Corps' Combat Hunter Program Can Save Your Life* (New York: Black Irish Books, 2014).
4 Klaus Wille, "Tudor Said to Close Singapore Trading Desk Amid Global Cuts", *Bloomberg*, 26 September 2016, at https://www.bloomberg.com/news/articles/2016-09-25/tudor-said-to-close-singapore-trading-desk-amid-global-job-cuts.

PART II
VISIONS FROM THE TRENCHES

Chapter 6

GETTING YOUR RHYTHM BACK: AN INTERVIEW WITH PAUL TUDOR JONES

Paul Tudor Jones was my idol when I was young. I read about him often in books and the financial news, and discovered his work in both his thriving hedge fund company and the charitable Robin Hood Foundation. I got to meet him personally in 2010, and have since been star-struck by his energetic persona, inquisitive nature and kind words. The next five years working as a money manager for Tudor were the best days of my trading career.

I've learned a lot from your stories. When I was turning 40, all my trades didn't work. You hit the same tough patch when you were 40, and you went down all the way to trade just one contract at a time and got your rhythm back. Can you share what happened then, and how you came back out from that hole?

Paul: Well, I think trading is much like any skill. It requires a process – or rather, a plan, a process and then repetition.

So when someone is trading poorly, their process is broken. You have to go back and look at the process, and I like to do that with as few concerns as possible while I'm doing it. To take the pressure off, I go back and trade in really, really tiny, micro-lot sizes, just to be able to make sure that my process is good.

In trading, there are four key categories. These are your alpha generation; your portfolio construction; your execution, which can maybe be the most important; and then your risk management. You have to get all four of these components right. Together, they all add up to a trading process.

What I do when I'm in a slump is to take the pressure off, then go back to first principles and make sure I get my process right. It's much like a golf swing, a tennis stroke or the right gun mount, trigger press and follow-through. It all boils down to making sure that you're onboarding and implementing best practices for your particular style of trading.

So it's mainly just getting back that same process that you've actually missed. Have you faced a more difficult situation after that? Perhaps even a non-work example?

Paul: Well, I'm involved in a lot of philanthropic causes. One thing I find in any organisation is it's going to be very cyclic. It's really hard to maintain a high standard of excellence at all times.

You're going to go through ups and downs, and with each one of them you're going to go through a slump. If you look at my lifetime Sharpe ratio, it's probably around 1.5, but there are times where I'm trading really well, and I'll have one year of Sharpe 3. When I'm trading really poorly, it will be from 0.2 to 0.4.

There's great amplitude in so much of everything in life – in your marriage, in your relationship, in your work. With that amplitude comes cyclicality. When things don't work out, you just have to take the time and you have to get invested in getting those things right. A lot of that just requires, again, going back to first principles.

The one thing that I found in 1992–1993, when I went down to trading one contract, my trading style had totally changed from the 1980s, and I wasn't even aware of it. I went from being the best trend trader in the whole world to a reversal trader, and it all happened without any conscious decision. I really was unaware until one of my associates, Spencer Lampert, pointed it out to me.

So you can, without even knowing, change in so many aspects of your personality. That's why a lot of this requires really good management and metrics. You must have a plan and process, and stick with them.

I'm sure you do a lot of looking back, right? Did you try to look back and see what was that strike, that moment when you changed?
Paul: As I grew in assets, it became more difficult to get a really good position on an uptrend. For instance, it could be because the liquidity, transaction or friction costs were so high. I was trying to buy up and resell down, and after a while, I got tired of having to pay through the nose and then be wrong.

The friction costs were so great that, without even knowing it, I came to prefer trading on limits rather than the market. I ended up becoming a reversal trader, because I was so focused on trading on limits that the only times I would get filled all the way was when counter-trend trading, and quite often I was flat-out wrong. That's why you must be conscious of externalities.

I think trading is no different from any other business. You have to have a business plan. You have to have an approach. You have to be disciplined. You have to be systematic.

When you think about it, it's a lot like playing a sport. Whether it's soccer or football, you need a game plan. Every time you play or go and trade, things can be different. Your plan will be subject to externalities – in the case of sports, what the other team is doing.

In the case of trading, you must adapt to the external environment, and what central banks or central governments are doing that you didn't anticipate. You have to modify, react and execute.

At the end of the day, I think anybody who's really, really good in anything they pursue is going to have a really technical, systematic, analytical, mathematical, scientific way of approaching it. Otherwise, they're not going to be successful. Anyone who thinks they can do it from their gut is going to end up losing out to someone who did the analysis.

In 2014, I was down four per cent, and you asked me to do an exercise to check my execution. You said to check all my trades with the "end of day" closing rate and calculate what the P&L would be. I did and realised that I would've been up seven per cent, had I traded at the "end of day" closing rate. So execution is definitely important.

You also told me that you directed your execution team to ask you, "Paul, is it a hard trade?" before doing it.

Paul: I'm still 100 per cent invested in that process. It's the most important thing you can possibly do because the reason why only a handful of people are successful is that Mr Market and Ms Market are sirens. They always ask you to do the wrong thing, because what is obvious is obviously wrong.

They ask you to buy when things look the best, and they ask you to sell when things look the worst. It's really, really hard to stay calm, and have the discipline to not get sucked into these traps. That's really what they are! It's just a trap.

The markets are the same way all the time. They're always asking, "Oh, please, please, things look so terrible. Please sell me," or "Things look so great. Please buy me." And, of course, the second you do, you mark the high or the low.

Would you like to share how you felt when you found out that your daughter was infected by COVID-19? How did you overcome that fear, and how is she doing right now?

Paul: She's doing great. I really wasn't that worried because, even at the time, it just hadn't impacted young people that much. She was in her 20s, healthy as she could possibly be and a great athlete, so I wasn't that worried. When I get worried, obviously, it would be for somebody over the age of 70 or so. Fortunately, I haven't had that experience.

So COVID is going to be such an interesting case study when it's all over. We're going to look at the benefit costs of shut down versus other approaches. I don't know what the answer is, and I don't think there's a black or white answer. It's probably something in between.

But it's going to be really, really interesting. Think about all the different approaches that all the countries are taking, and consider their GDP and their recovery; as well as how fast the vaccine is developed and delivered. You see how many lives could have been saved versus the economic costs, and then you must somehow try to quantify the cost of death for someone over the age of 80. It's going to be the most interesting sociological issue to tackle.

On a lighter note, Paul, you told me when you hire someone for a job, you don't just consider if they will do well with you, but you also care about the cost of them giving up their current job. The more qualified a person, the higher that cost could be.

That forever changed the way I recruit people because I keep thinking about them leaving their job at every interview that I give now. Where do you get these insights from, and what do you look for when you hire people?

Paul: Everyone is internally analysing the costs and benefits of pursuing the various opportunities open to them. When I think about someone who's going to join Tudor, I'm always trying to understand from their standpoint what they're giving up versus what they think they're gaining. Clearly, you want there to be a compelling future for both them and for Tudor.

When I look for someone to hire, it depends on the position because each position requires a different skill. But in a trader, I'm generally looking for somebody with a real attitude and passion for math and numbers.

That can manifest itself in a bunch of different ways. It could be coding, it could be computer science, it could be physics. It could be game playing. It could be backgammon or bridge. You want someone who just enjoys problem-solving because, at the end of the day, all trading is problem-solving, where the math and the probabilities are just critically important. I'd say that's where you want to start.

The next thing for anyone successful in virtually any type of trading or research role is the ability to frame. Framing is so important. Because you've got to be able to boil everything down into principal components. It's critical that you're able to understand the foundational elements of any kind of proposition facing you.

So you want to be able to get right past the noise, right past all the bells and whistles. You want to understand the proposition at its essence.

The same thing applies when you're hiring somebody. At the end of the day, what is the proposition with that particular person? Is it their attitude or their skill sets? How are they going to deal in that kind of work ecosystem we all exist in?

The ideal person is someone who's really good with numbers and analytically very fast, and then can write well. Someone who can write well obviously has kind of a logic model that allows them to organise things in a coherent process, and that's a basic skill.

It's the basis of any business plan. There's a start, a middle and a finish, and trade is exactly the same way. You've got to see your trade all the way, and learn where it'll be six months, a year or 18 months from now, and decide how you'll deal with that journey along the way.

That's the next hardest part about trading. I can't tell you how many times I've been right at first, then screwed up a move. I'm sure many other people have been the same way.

Which is more important, getting in or out of a trade?
Paul: I think it's getting out. I think of myself as the most conservative investor on earth, and I'm probably too quick to take losses. But the question is, can you just survive to live another day?

My first boss, when I first started trading at 21, was Eli Tullis. I asked him if I could open a trading account.

"The answer is no, and here's why," he said. "The market is going to be there 30 years from now, that I can guarantee you. The question is, will *you* be there? You need to take your time and understand the game first. Trading 'right now' is not going to help you develop an approach."

So I would say that the one thing I learned was that the markets were indeed there 30 years later. Fifteen years after that, they're still there. The trick is that *you're* going to have difficult, challenging times. Will you come out of them with enough capital to exploit an opportunity you saw earlier?

That's the one thing I would say. If you're just patient enough, you'll have perfect vision – be it after a month, six months or a year or longer. And that's the beauty of our business; you can just leverage yourself and make a killing. It's just that you have to make sure you're in the game, with enough in the bank to exploit the opportunity.

You've told me to think about my family before taking some big risk. Do you think one should be taking more risks in their life and trading instead?
Paul: I would say if I have one regret, it's that I probably haven't been aggressive enough. But I'm really happy where I am, so I'm not going to complain.

But you always wish you could have done better. I think *ex post*, if you know your lifetime Sharpe would be 1.5, would you be taking a lot more risks than you would be if you didn't know that? I don't know if I'll keep trading well for the rest of my life.

But I know that being conservative has gotten me this far, so I'm going to stay with it. It's just who I am – I think by the time in you're in your 40s, you have a pretty good idea of your personality. I do believe that old maxim: "You can't teach an old dog new tricks." It's really, really hard to change. I have seen it.

You never see a new trader come onto the scene all of a sudden who is around the same age as you. You've either, by that point in time, developed a successful approach or stopped altogether.

I don't care who it is. It's really hard starting at age 50 to learn all the skills to be able to compete at the top levels. I've yet to see anyone who suddenly opened a hedge fund at age 50 and was really successful.

During a life-changing event, you just can't trade, right?
Paul: No one has ever traded successfully in those times. When my mother passed away, I tried trading through it, only to be down six per cent in that month, which was a huge drawdown at that point in time. Emotional impact does have consequences.

Funerals and divorces are horrific, but births are life-changing, and either way, if you're a discretionary trader, they're going to impact you.

You're not going to be able to look at things analytically, and stay rationally focused during those periods of emotional distraction. It's just not going to happen.

If you see any of your portfolio managers not working out, how would you positively encourage them to do something else? This is also a question arising from the COVID-19 crisis, whereby a lot of jobs are not coming back. How do you tell them to do something else?

Paul: Well, it's funny how I've become so philosophical. Life is a journey. Good Lord, when I think about how many different people I've met along the way, how many different things I've done, and even how my trading style has changed ... well, when someone starts trading, and it doesn't work out, that's probably the odds.

Some 85 per cent of small businesses fail, and trading is probably like that, too. It's just part of the journey, and I think you've got to look at it philosophically. Remember breakups as a teenager and all the heartbreak? Those who recover and keep looking for the right person eventually get them.

That's what I encourage people to do. You've got a hell of a life ahead of you. You're looking for the right thing, and this is part of that sampling process that you go through to ultimately find the right place for you. It will definitely come over time, so long as you approach everything with a great level of energy, passion and rationality.

Thirty years ago, you founded Robin Hood. You must have seen countless children coming out of poverty. Can you share any examples, and what do they have in common?
Paul: There's a guy named Yusuf George who works at JUST Capital. He's an example of nature versus nurture, and he was selected for my I Have a Dream Program back in the 1990s. He had the golden touch in the beginning and was going to be outstanding at whatever he did. What I remember is that he was incredibly curious.

You can already see these characteristics at age ten to 15 or 16. You have a good idea who's going to be outstanding and who's not. Much of this is genetic, and they self-select into various pursuits. They're going to bring greatness with them.

I think for professional jobs that require leadership and intellectual capacity, you see so much of it early on. By the time you're 15 or 16, you already know so much of what you will eventually know, because early childhood is the best time for cognitive skills. Pretty much the entire roadmap is done by the time you're three or four years old.

Nurture takes over from there and those kids build on that great base. They just find a way to reach the right places to take them on to the next level.

When we met in your office 18 months ago, I told you that one day I was going to start managing money again. You replied, "Hold on. You've got to be the big fish in a small pond."

Why is it important advice? Do you think it's still important?
Paul: What's happened in the financial markets is that the world's intellectual talents have made it into an interconnected

system. Back in the 1980s and 1990s, traders didn't have to be the smartest at the table – now, the most intelligent dominate the industry. The domain expertise required to be successful today is so much greater by orders of magnitude.

So my advice would be to find something where you truly are one of the three or four most informed principals in that particular space. If you know it thoroughly, then you have a reasonable chance of doing well in it.

If you try to be a generalist and you try to compete with all these extraordinary people, it's going to be a real challenge. Looking at the way the world is shaking out, the specialists are definitely winning the game.

More and more institutions are getting into Bitcoin and Ethereum. What are the differences in strategy on trading digital assets compared to trading traditional financial markets?
Paul: Trading crypto is very different from virtually any other financial instrument primarily because of its volatility. It is about eight times more volatile than the S&P500 and I don't think most investors take that into consideration. The corrections in crypto will be breathtaking. It reminds one of silver in that the commercial demand is very limited and so when a speculative washout takes hold, you wonder if there is a bottom.

Paul, I really appreciate your time, could you give me three words to describe the future of cryptocurrencies?
Paul: Up, up, and away!

Chapter 7

MANUFACTURING LUCK: AN INTERVIEW WITH VISHAL AGRAWAL

Vishal and I met when we were working together in the same bank in 2017. A year later, he joined BlackRock as an investor in the Global Emerging Markets Equities Team within the Fundamental Active Equity division. This interview explains our relationship and, more importantly, he shares examples from his own life of good luck being a choice we make.

Suppose it's been a hectic day at the market, and equities have sold off three per cent and then five per cent. It's like the biggest one-day drop in many years. Everyone is saying that it's a VAR shock. Everything is going to go. The dollar is higher against all currencies and suddenly lower – it's the noisiest you've ever heard the floor.

How do you normally react in the first place in such a scene?
Vishal: You know, over the years I've learned that there is a difference between signal and noise. The biggest favour that you can do for yourself is to be calm and assess the situation

first. Going with the first impulsive reaction can cause you to blunder.

We're all uncomfortable seeing panic unfold. There's the temptation to pull the trigger really hard and say, "I'm out of here."

But if you don't know the facts, really, I think it's good to go and grasp the facts first rather than jumping impulsively, because impulsive behaviour in the markets typically ends up being painful. So don't act until and unless you have the facts clear.

I've learnt this from you and others: don't build castles on borrowed conviction. The first thing I do in a crisis is to calm down and quickly take a couple of minutes to get the facts straight. Then I make the decisive decisions.

Because in moments like this, what separates men from boys is not only acting quickly, but acting decisively. And acting decisively can only happen once you have your facts right. If you act based on nothing more than your conviction, often you're going to be stopped out on both sides.[1] So it's better to have your facts correct, rather than just trading impulsively.

Yeah, I think that applies for all situations. Once you panic, you tend to make wrong decisions. You are a successful trader in BlackRock now. Can you share your successes?
Vishal: I'm in the portfolio management side. I don't know how to define success, but I do know it is reflected by longevity. The next 20 years will decide whether I'm successful, or just an average Joe out there.

Notice that Charles Darwin didn't say it's the *strongest* who survives, but the most *adaptable*. In the two years of my career at BlackRock, I've been extremely adaptive – situations have changed, from the US-China trade war to the equities meltdown of 18 December 2018, then the Phase One trade deal and, as of this writing, COVID-19.

I think what makes people really grounded in this market is being humble, being curious and, most importantly, being adaptive. No one can say, "It's my way or the highway," because the screen is always right. We just need to adhere to making the most of what comes our way.

What I've tried to do is to build on my strengths. One of them is fundamental analysis, particularly in the medium term. And my weakness is that I don't know how to treat the noise well or do very short-term stuff. So I try to stick with medium-term commissions, and size my trades and hedge accordingly. That means I try to build a portfolio based on my strengths, and try to be cognisant of my weaknesses.

Yeah, I totally agree with that, Vishal. What drives you to trade? Is it the money?

Vishal: No. I mean, money is one factor. In life it's like a scorecard at the end of the day. But what drives me is intellectual curiosity. When I got injured in 2004 and started losing my sight, my world was lost in darkness.

Since 2008 when I started my career, the most amazing part of our business is that it's like a business of businesses. Absolutely everything runs on merit. For some time you can fool someone and do something, but in this business, the only thing which defines long-term success is merit. And that is based on intellectual stimulation, luck, curiosity. And money is an outcome of that.

What drives me is there's something new every day. It's never a dull day – our lives are so interesting! We can read so much. We can meet interesting people. We can evaluate a lot of situations. Every day makes you humble because every time you make newer and newer mistakes, you learn from them. Your brain becomes almost like a mosaic machine, connecting the dots. And we're all bonded by our own experiences.

As long as we remain true to ourselves that we will have to be agile and change when the facts change, I think it's a great business. For someone like me who's genuinely very curious about life, I think I couldn't be in a better business.

One thing I really admire about you is that you've put your disability behind. Lots of people would just say, "Oh, I can't see anything. I can't hear anything. Please help me." But for the first few questions in this interview, you didn't even mention your impairment. So I really admire you for that.

You became blind in your teens. Can you tell me what happened?

Vishal: Yeah, sure. Hoe Lon, to your point, I believe that I'm an investor who happens to be blind, not a blind guy who happens to be an investor. My skills, my merit, my performance should be the deciding factor in my career, not the other way around.

My life has been a roller coaster, as you know. In 2004, I was about to go to the US for my undergraduate studies. The year before I had been hit by a cricket ball, but we didn't know for a couple of months that I had been injured. A vein in my eye was affected, reducing blood circulation there and I started losing my sight.

I couldn't go to the US, so I did my undergrad in India. From 2004 to 2008, I ended up losing 80 per cent of my sight, with the world lost in darkness. The only question in front of me was "why me?"

Why me? What had I done wrong? There was no hope.

I was about to end my life, and indeed I tried ending my life for six weeks. Fortunately, I failed. That's when my parents jumped to my rescue, and they gave me two principles of life which I think are the real bedrock of my existence.

First, if you try, there is a probability you'll succeed. If you don't, there's a guarantee you'll fail. And second, what goes around comes around. If you're nice and empathetic to people, it's a favour that you do for yourself, because everything comes back in various shapes and forms.

So I try and live on both of these principles today. Like starting my own hedge fund in April 2008, weathering the global financial crisis. For the next three years, I had a five-fold return, and I ended up going to business school in India from 2011 to 2013.

I didn't get a job while on campus, and wrote more than 5,000 cold emails. In the end, I got a job at Standard Chartered Bank, where we met on the global macro-trading desk. I had a great time over the five years there, and moved into the buying side of BlackRock in 2018.

It's been a roller coaster ride. Every time I think my life is going to be stable, something comes and hits me. So what I've learned over the years is to come back to my parents' principles. The outcome I leave aside, because you're not in control of many things in your life. In the markets, you can work, say, ten times harder than anyone else and still not have the results in your favour. There's always an element of randomness or luck, whatever you want to call it. But we keep trying.

How do we deal with luck? Here we return to my parents' second principle – that what goes around comes around. Being kind and helpful to others is helping yourself in a practical sense. That's called manufactured luck. Someone I've helped may or may not help me in return, but the world is an equaliser.

People come back and help me in different forms, like you did as my super boss at Standard Chartered. We became friends. That's like manufactured luck; perhaps I helped someone else and ended up meeting you. One of the most incredible days of my life was when you got me a meeting with one of my top three investors, Paul Tudor Jones.

You gave it to me without my even asking, and that's really what life offers you. What goes around, comes around.

So these are the two things that I really try and be true to. Hopefully, you and I will scale greater heights in life.

Before that when you were in Standard Chartered, I was reading a lot of your emails, full of great insights and articles. I had no idea who these emails were from and asked around. Your hard work brought that opportunity on yourself, to be discovered.

I can't picture what it's like to live in complete darkness. How did you handle that moment?

Vishal: I won't say that it's not tough, or it's not hard. At some moments in life, you genuinely feel scared and you feel fearful, but there's a saying that courage is a kite that flies in contradicting winds. The people who win are the ones who overcome their fears.

So I kind of told myself, "Get up, Vishal!" The only difference between me and failure is persistence. I'm not extraordinary or smart, I just think I'm super persistent and curious ... and uprightly honest. I've definitely felt completely lost in the middle of trading, but I catch myself and remind myself not to give up. As long as I don't, life doesn't end. It's like a boxing match – the loser isn't the one who gets hit hard or falls down, but the one who refuses to get back up.

I tell myself to give it my best, and try until my last breath. That's the only thing I tell myself every time I get knocked out. In the markets, we get knocked out every day ... but each new day is a new chance. When times get tough, we need to haul ourselves back and try again. That's the difference between the super successful and the merely average.

Can you cry?
Vishal: Yeah, I cry. It happened a lot ten years back, but it's much less now. I try and be rational. In markets, I try and be non-emotional; in business, I use my emotions but try not to be emotional. But of course, we all are humans. I cry. I have my low moments.

That's okay ... but past a point, you wipe the tears away and make it work. Again, we'll all be treated unfairly. We'll all get dealt bad hands in life. But the most successful ask themselves:

"This is the situation. How can I fix it?"

People who are most solution-oriented are, I think, the ones who change their lives ... and the world. I aspire to be solution-oriented, solving problems rather than letting them discourage me. Solutions drive people forward, and that's how they advance. Fail fast, as you say, but fall forward! That's how we keep growing and delivering to be successful.

What frustrates you most about being visually impaired?
Vishal: Some of what frustrates me is people's attitude. I think the biggest disability that each one of us has is a bad attitude. We've got to start respecting people for who they are rather than their appearance, their disabilities. That's why I don't tell people I'm sight-impaired, and anyone who hasn't met or read about me wouldn't know this.

I just start by saying I'm an investor who happens to be sight-impaired. I'm not a sight-impaired guy who happens to be an investor.

But yet, people will either pity me and say, "Oh, what a poor chap", or they'll put me on a pedestal and call me superhuman. Neither is true, and neither lets them befriend me – you can't befriend someone you pity or someone you perceive as a superhuman. You become friends with normal people.

I am a normal person who wants to be normal. Each one of us is special in our own right, so just treat me normally. We all have our own unique skill sets and pros and cons. Bill Gates, Steve Jobs, Mark Zuckerberg, George Soros, Paul Tudor Jones, Stan Druckenmiller, Warren Buffett and Charlie Munger are all normal people with skill sets that are in demand.

If you treat people with respect, I think that just makes the ecosystem very positive. That's all I ask of others. It's your attitude, not your aptitude, which decides your altitude in your life.

Amazing. Can you give us a bit more detail on how you stay positive yourself? What are you grateful for?
Vishal: I try and tell myself the choices that I have. You can be positive or negative, you can find a solution or break down. Only the first will help the situation, and if you keep trying to solve the problem, you'll seldom fail in life. The second path may seem easier, but you will rarely succeed taking it.

Obviously, as Buffett says, you're the average of five people who are in your life. I'm blessed and grateful for people like you in my life. When you're frustrated and falling into the groove of pessimism and giving up, it's the people around you who will pull you out, if they can. You need that ecosystem, so you choose your friends very carefully.

That's very true. Can you walk us through how you trade on a day-to-day basis? How is it different from other traders?
Vishal: The only difference is that people look at screens and I hear the screen. The software is a screen reader which is now available in all devices, whether it's your smartphone, tablet or laptop.

I can use Bloomberg like you. I read messages. I can type on the computer like you and anyone else. The only difference is that you read the screen with your eyes, while I have a headset locked to my computer which reads out stuff to me at lightning speed. That's a system I've practiced and perfected over the last ten years. Hopefully, I'll keep getting better.

Our brains work with input-process-output, but it's just that my input is sound while yours is visual. Other than my input being via sound, my process and output are like yours, I can type on my computer and phone.

To give a quick scientific analogy: our brains process two billion signals a day – half of that is visual, but because I can't see, 50 per cent of my brain capacity is unused. The elastic mind theory says that your brain capacity can slowly be expanded, so I try and expand it. I don't know how much I've expanded it, say from 1 billion to 1.2 billion, 1.4 billion, I don't know. So even if I've gone to 1.4 billion, that means my brain capacity has gone up 40 per cent.

And not all your senses go up in the same magnitude. Some people really get better at touch, while others get better in vision, taste, sound or speech. The process is all about evolution. I'm trying to push harder and fail forward. It's scientifically proven, and movies like *Daredevil* and *The Matrix* which show people seeing with their eyes closed and comprehending what's around them are based on reality. It's all about pushing yourself forward.

Do you think you are disadvantaged in your job by not being able to see? And how?
Vishal: Everyone has their own strengths and weaknesses. I think my weakness is that I can't be a short-term trader. I can't trade in the next two hours because I can't see charts, images and graphs.

This means I can't trade noise. I'm a more medium-term, fundamental-oriented person who knows what his strength is. I think that's what sometimes becomes a challenge, but each to his own. Some people are great at trading in the short term, but often those who are, aren't the right people to trade medium-term. The reverse is also true, those who are really good at trading medium-term are not that great in the short term.

And obviously there are a few gifted people like you who can trade in both the medium term and short term. Some of the trading legends whom we all know can trade in the short, medium and long term. I can't, so I think that's one of my drawbacks.

Over the years, I've realised it's sometimes good to know what your weaknesses are, so that you're cognisant of them and can improve life around them. I think I'm too young right now to make such a comment, but I think in the 33 years of my life, I realise that many people are miserable because they don't know their weaknesses, or don't really want to work on them if they do.

I think once you know what your weakness is, you should try and push your strengths, and make sure you're recognised for your strengths. Try to minimise the grey zones where you have to deal with a lot of your weaknesses.

We don't have to know everything in life, though we need to know what we need to know.

Those are great skills to have, knowing and working around your weaknesses. Not being able to see has probably shaped you to laser-focus on some other areas. But do you have a different thought

process from your ability to focus? Who are your mentors, and what are some of the important lessons you've learned from them?
Vishal: It starts with the two principles I talked about earlier – try and never give up, because once you try, there's a probability you'll succeed. If you don't, there's a guarantee you'll fail; and second, what goes around comes around. Be nice and empathetic to people, because niceness goes a long way.

Third, accept and appreciate what you know and what you don't know. Focus on your strengths and be cognisant of your weaknesses.

Finally, the most important thing (and one I learnt pretty late in life) is to just say that I don't know some things. Sometimes we want to look smart and fear looking bad, so we don't admit or accept that we don't know things.

If you don't know, it's okay because not everyone is supposed to know everything all the time. So sometimes, accepting with humility that we don't know is what really makes us fail fast and fall forward. Because once you say, "I don't know" or "I'm stupid", you start the process of learning. Until that point where you finally accept that you don't know something, you don't really work hard to understand it.

Nowadays in meetings, if I don't know an answer, I don't try to pretend that I know it. I raise my hand and say, "Can you explain it to me?" It might look stupid and people might judge me, but that's okay. They can judge me and call me stupid once, but after that moment I've learnt what I need to know. Because if I keep quiet, even if they think I'm smart, I'm genuinely stupid for the rest of my life.

So I think accepting your flaws and embracing them, to

work on them if need be, is having clear focus. It's like the Pareto Principle: 20 per cent of your activities make up 80 per cent of your life. I try and focus on what I know, and I don't try to pretend I know something when I don't.

Yeah, that's a good point. And then think about it – if it's the other way around and you say you know something that you don't, it becomes a real problem at some point.

What are some of your aspirations and how are you working towards them?

Vishal: I only have two goals in life, one professional and the other personal. The professional one is to be a successful investor and hopefully, like other successful investors, have a long-standing career and build something of my own. With friends and mentors around, I'm building a track record and honing my skills every day.

The personal one is to be healthy and help my family grow, ensuring that they have a comfortable life.

But beyond that, I genuinely want to create awareness in the world, and make it a more inclusive place. I truly believe that inclusion in action leads to diversity, not just of colour and ability, but of thought, deed and character. Different markets have evolved, and people of different backgrounds bring different things to our table. That can only move us forward.

I'm genuinely grateful to all the people in my life at various stages who have really helped me. You, obviously, are one who has helped me to go and propel forward. Do I have an ability to help them back? Not really, but I can extend gratitude by helping a lot of underprivileged people out there.

So I try and speak at various forums globally *pro bono* – to create awareness that technology is empowering inclusion, and to ensure that people are hired based on ability and not discarded based on disability. I've run marathons over the last four years raising funds for various causes, like cancer kids, autism, Down syndrome, women's empowerment and child education.

It's a small world and we all need to do our bit. Each one of us can be the change maker out there. I'm hoping that I can do my small bit, and also motivate a few others to be change makers. It's about making the change, not the numbers. If we're only able to change like five people's lives in our life, that's still five people who matter.

What advice do you have for people who have been affected by the Bitcoin crash? (This was January 2020.)
Vishal: Go back to the drawing board, and analyse your facts and fundamentals. If you truly believe the situation is an anomaly, rework your strategy and come back in full force.

You don't fail when markets turn around you. You fail when you don't manage your risk adequately, or when you give up. If you believe in the asset class, which I truly do, you just need to rework your strategy. Reassess how you can make real value-add back, and invest double your time and energy. Really think how you can make it back.

Because, as an asset class, I genuinely believe that crypto and Bitcoin are here to stay because of the ascent of money, the parallel universe. Given that central bank easing is really the need of the government, we need a different asset class which is truly agnostic.

What are your thoughts on the future of cryptocurrency? How do you see it playing out?

Vishal: My fundamental belief is that money was invented because people needed a standardised asset for barter, and that has been going on for ages. Gold was considered a standard but like 50 years back, the gold standard was abolished. In the last ten years after the global financial crisis, money has lost much of its value in massive central bank easing.

With blockchain, you can actually have a ledger account to trace where things are going. Crypto and Bitcoin are alternative forms of this – as you know, money has had centuries to evolve and change. It wasn't always the same money that we are using today. It keeps evolving.

My fundamental belief is that crypto is here to stay. Will it change its shape and form? Absolutely.

We need to be agile. We need to be dynamic. And we need to be value creative because, as a matter of fact, this is an asset class which is evolving in its early stages and is here to stay and, most importantly, it will stay and grow disproportionately in a very rapid, accelerated pace. It will have its own pulls and pushes, but people who kind of stay true to their convictions are the ones who will be really rewarded in the long term.

Endnotes

1 To be "stopped out" is to be stopped from trading by a stop-loss order, with the implication that there has been a loss, and being stopped on "both sides" means a trader gets stopped out on the positions of price going up as well as going down. It means the trader will lose money either way.

Chapter 8

THE FUTURE OF DECENTRALISED FINANCE: AN INTERVIEW WITH LOI LUU

Loi is one of the three founders of decentralised exchange Kyber Network. One of the top smart contract coders when cryptocurrencies were heating up, he led a small team to one of the most successful ICOs of 2017.

I was lucky enough to be hired as one of the two Executive Advisers. I shared my experience in open outcry trading, in which the "locals" (that is, the traders in the exchange) played an integral part of the liquidity in a market.

Kyber's ICO was the first to raise two sets of funds, one for the build-up of the exchange and the other for a liquidity reserve. This latter use provided the last resort of prices, like a local trader would in the days of open outcry trading.

You've come a long way. I still remember that coffee we had in the NUS canteen in 2017, when you talked about the mining project you were working on and your dreams of creating what we have today – DeFi. Why does it matter?

Loi: Decentralised Finance (DeFi) has a huge potential to disrupt the traditional financial system, by simply introducing a completely new way for people to participate in finance. Since financial intermediaries can be removed for the first time, there is an opportunity for greater financial inclusion. In addition, transactions happen in a transparent environment, the public blockchains, so financial activities in DeFi are less prone to fraud and counterparty risks.

With that in mind, there were two main motivations for my co-founders and me to build Kyber Network as a key liquidity infrastructure for the DeFi space.

Firstly, we realised that DeFi cannot succeed without trustless and non-custodial value exchange. Centralised cryptocurrency trading required a lot of trust in the platform owners and was a hassle for end users. They need to deposit their assets to centralised exchanges, and wait for confirmation of receipt before being able to trade.

Trades are also not fully transparent and verifiable. Moreover, there have been many high-profile hacks on centralised exchanges over the past few years, like what happened to Mt Gox in 2014 and Upbit in 2019, with millions of dollars' worth of crypto assets lost. When your crypto assets are residing in these custodial services, you don't have control over them, and risk losing them to hacks or fraud.

Secondly, DeFi applications require trustless on-chain liquidity to fully leverage the benefits of permissionless composability. This means different decentralised applications and protocols can interact and work together simultaneously to create innovative use cases that were previously impossible. It's one of the main growth drivers for DeFi.

Such frictionless innovation requires on-chain liquidity from the decentralised ecosystem, since applications and protocols cannot interact with centralised platforms (such as centralised exchanges) without breaking their trust assumption.

We couldn't find any convenient solution for the average user to swap tokens securely in DeFi. There was also no solution supporting on-chain liquidity for the smart contract ecosystem, as incumbent platforms were hybrids that still involved a central server.

That motivated us to develop Kyber Network, a fully on-chain and permissionless protocol meant to facilitate seamless decentralised token exchange and provide liquidity for DeFi. Any application can integrate with the liquidity protocol, with no gatekeepers dictating innovation – a very important growth driver for DeFi.

Trades on Kyber are also fully transparent and verifiable. By using Kyber as their transaction layer, projects in DeFi will in turn be able to gain access to on-chain liquidity and achieve their full potential.

I am eternally grateful to you for offering me the opportunity to work with you on creating Kyber. I was just a finance guy with no full-time job, and looking for a break. Can you recount how the experience was on your side? Building a decentralised exchange, with our winning factor, alongside a strong reserve to manage the liquidity.

Loi: Meeting you was a serendipitous moment! People like you are very important in the DeFi space as you have brought in traditional financial market expertise, and enabled us to build things that could serve professional traders and market makers who handle billions of US dollars.

Although our Kyber team had already developed the fundamental technology for creating a cutting-edge decentralised trading platform and liquidity protocol, we still required advice from veteran traders like you who could help us navigate the challenges and contribute to product design from a financial and trading perspective. You readily extended your help whenever we needed it, and we will always be appreciative of your contribution.

To date, Kyber has over 50 unique reserves (liquidity sources) connected to a large taker network of over 100 decentralised apps (or DApps), and these reserves have facilitated a cumulative trading volume of close to $3 billion. Building upon our team's in-depth knowledge of on-chain market making and Kyber's proven Fed Price Reserve (FPR) system, we also developed KyberPRO, the first end-to-end framework designed for professionals to efficiently market make on the blockchain and gain access to DeFi. These milestones were only possible through the combined efforts of our team, community and expert advisors from various fields.

Let's tie everything back together. How is Kyber still a DeFi champion, and how popular is it at the start of the 2020s?
Loi: Kyber was initially constructed to be a straightforward decentralised platform for seamless token exchange that was

accessible to as many end users as possible. In 2017, more than 25,000 people participated in Kyber's token sale and used the platform across multiple interfaces.

Subsequently, with the advent of DeFi and permissionless composability, there was an explosion in the number of new use cases. Most of these use cases needed on-chain liquidity that was easily accessible by smart contracts, and allowed a trustless relationship between providers and makers.

To address this critical need in the DeFi space, we realised very early on that Kyber needed to be what it is today, an on-chain liquidity protocol that allows *both* open contribution of liquidity from token holders and open integration by any application to power their crucial liquidity and transaction needs. With Kyber's liquidity infrastructure, transactional flows can happen atomically and in a single step between multiple parties, enabling instant and seamless transactions between DApps, ecosystems and other use cases. Many DeFi use cases would otherwise be very difficult or impossible to achieve.

Currently, interest in DeFi is growing from strength to strength, and the total value locked in the DeFi space has even surpassed $14 billion! This could be attributed to the proliferation of stablecoins pegged to the US dollar such as DAI or USDC, which have gained popularity as a means to earn interest on lending platforms. In addition, more DeFi protocols and DApps are finally live on the mainnet and ready for adoption.

A large number of these DeFi use cases require on-chain liquidity. Since liquidity in the decentralised space is currently scattered among different on-chain liquidity sources, Kyber integrates liquidity providers (reserves) into one single endpoint for takers (DApps and end users) to easily access. When a taker requests a trade, the protocol will scan the entire network to find the reserve with the best price and take liquidity from that particular reserve.

For example, on lending platforms where users can deposit collateral to borrow assets for margin trading, Kyber can be integrated to seamlessly liquidate collateral at competitive prices, whenever margin calls occur. Kyber can also be used on asset management platforms to help users automatically rebalance their token portfolios based on predetermined investment strategies.

Kyber's fully on-chain design allows for full transparency and verifiability in the matching engine, as well as seamless composability with DApps, all of which are not possible with off-chain or hybrid approaches. Kyber's flexible reserve system also connects to a large variety of liquidity providers that make it uniquely capable of supporting sophisticated schemes and catering to the various needs of DeFi DApps and financial institutions. Not surprisingly, Kyber became the most used and popular DeFi protocol in 2019.

We are incredibly fortunate to have a global and diverse community that has always supported and believed in us through ups and downs since Kyber's inception. All these gave us the confidence and insights to open up the core platform so that it can be utilised in a much more expansive way.

Let me slot in a personal question. Looking back on your life, would you do anything differently? Why or why not?

Loi: Perhaps purchase or mine more Ether when Ethereum first launched? Just kidding!

I think judging our actions by hindsight is not a very constructive way of living, so I am happy for everything that I have done so far. Being a scientific problem-solver at heart, it has been very appealing for me to have the opportunity to conduct research, push the boundaries of technology, and contribute to the field of computer science by creating something valuable via my own startup, as opposed to being an employee fulfilling someone else's agenda. I am grateful for the journey that I have gone through so far, and even more grateful to have the support from friends and advisors like you.

Throughout this roller coaster of an entrepreneurship journey, there has been a lot of stress due to the never-ceasing challenges I faced on a daily basis. But my various life experiences have helped me step out of my comfort zone, made me more independent and resourceful, and contributed to my personal development. Ultimately, they have enabled me to make better decisions both in my personal life and when it comes to leading Kyber Network today.

What could have been done better? I certainly would think about preparing the company better, financially and mentally, to be more resilient to the crypto market changes. Right after our fundraising, there was a long "winter" in the cryptocurrency market that affected our company's runway and our team's mentality and confidence significantly. Though we fared better than many other teams, we certainly think it could have been handled differently to smoothen the impact on everyone in the team.

What are the shortcomings of DeFi?
Loi: DeFi is like a double-edged sword. Its open nature allows endless possibilities for innovation and value creation but, at the same time, this makes it a hotbed for scams and hacks. New users are often fearful of using DApps due to the many security attacks that have previously occurred. Some $70 million was lost in exploits during October and November 2020 alone!

This severely curtailed adoption, and the problem is often exacerbated by a poor user interface and experience on many platforms.

In addition, the DeFi landscape is fragmented, with many DApps and chains existing in their own individual silos. For greater liquidity and usability, there needs to be a way to bridge liquidity across these platforms and allow frictionless exchange of value.

At Kyber, we have taken steps to address these issues. We regularly educate our users on the benefits of decentralised technologies over centralised ones, and have published over 60 videos and 100 articles explaining Kyber's protocol and initiatives. Kyber's smart contracts have undergone multiple audits, and the protocol aggregates liquidity from multiple on-chain sources to give better rates and liquidity to takers (DApps and end users) via a single endpoint.

In addition, our in-house token swap platform KyberSwap.com is well-known for its great user interface and experience, and we continue to iterate and ensure our technical documentation is easily understood and used by developers. As part of a long-term objective to solve high gas fees during instances of network congestion, we have a dedicated team researching scaling solutions.

Overall, it isn't easy for a single project to overcome all the inherent challenges of DeFi on its own. A team effort is necessary, and ecosystem participants have to sometimes put aside their competition and work together to help drive DeFi adoption. A good example of an ecosystem-wide collaboration effort that Kyber helped to launch is the Wrapped Bitcoin (WBTC) initiative, in which over 40 different blockchain projects came together to bring Bitcoin liquidity to Ethereum. Today, over 117,700 WBTC ($2.17 billion) have been minted, and are used in DeFi apps on Ethereum.

As DeFi becomes increasingly popular, Kyber will continue to work with other pioneers to make blockchain and cryptocurrencies more usable in any application, on any smart contract-enabled blockchain.

What do you predict is the road ahead for DeFi?
Loi: I foresee that the DeFi space will continue to flourish. With DeFi, financial assets can now be recorded, managed and transferred in a way that is secure, trustless and transparent, without intermediaries. Important wealth-building and business tools such as applications involving loans, insurance, investments and other financial services will become much more accessible to people around the world. Anyone with an internet connection and a smartphone or laptop will be able to connect to the public blockchain network, use DeFi platforms and participate in the digital economy.

As more professionals from traditional finance start to

understand the value of DeFi, a brain drain of talent might also migrate towards DeFi startups. Specifically for Kyber, there will be a huge demand from professional market makers to market make on-chain, and with our new KyberPRO framework, we have the necessary tools for them to contribute liquidity to DeFi efficiently.

Personally, I am very confident that one day, blockchain and cryptocurrencies will become so embedded in our lives that people will not even notice it, just like how the Internet and smartphones operate today. The impact of DeFi will keep increasing as more people use smartphones and get more comfortable managing their finances online.

This is the future that Kyber aims to enable. We are building an on-chain liquidity protocol to facilitate the conversion of cryptocurrencies in the most trustless and secure manner. Our long-term goal is for Kyber to process most of the financial transactions for applications in the DeFi space.

Like all markets and most successful companies, Kyber has been through tough times. During the "crypto winter" when Ethereum lost 90 per cent of its valuation, what was on your mind? Did you think of giving up? Many did, irresponsibly, but you held on to your promises to your supporters. How hard was it?
Loi: We have been in this space for years and have experienced Ethereum's ups and downs many times. Occasionally we do look at the prices, but for the most part we focus on building and increasing adoption of Kyber, while growing the decentralised ecosystem together with other projects. We truly believe in the future of this space, and that decentralised finance will play an

important role in the global economy. Thus, we are not overly concerned with short-term fluctuations in the prices.

During the "crypto winter" phase, we laid out a lot of the foundational work for Kyber's protocol and taker network. For example, most of Kyber's integrations with other projects in the crypto space, such as HTC's blockchain phone, Trust Wallet and MyEtherWallet, were done much faster. Everyone understood that only purpose-driven building and shipping could save us all from the crypto winter.

I am also glad to be supported by a talented team who are unified in their passion for blockchain and Kyber's development. There is an old Chinese saying: "A single tree does not make a forest; a single string cannot make music." Great success can only be achieved with great teamwork, and our team constantly supports and encourages one another during challenging periods. Together, we are determined to enable decentralised finance, and create a world where any token is usable anywhere.

Have you thought about your legacy? What do you want to be remembered for?
Loi: For making a huge impact in global finance by pushing decentralised trading adoption around the world, together with the Kyber team.

It might seem too early for people my age to think about legacy (I'm not even 30 years old yet!) but being in this space for so long, we understand that the crypto space is still extremely immature. This is the best time for us to shape its future and make positive changes to the world. We, today, have the best shot anyone has had in decades to really push the incumbents in banking and finance to re-look at the financial system and improve their services, or at least drive greater innovation. That's the impact that I want to have in our world with the Kyber team.

Three words on cryptocurrency, what are they?
Loi: Innovative, open and limitless.

Chapter 9

CONQUERING FEAR AND STEPPING UP: AN INTERVIEW WITH JIMMY LIM

Jimmy started in the banking industry a few years later than I did. He climbed up the ladder rapidly and when we met, we were peers and had a similar path in our careers. We took a substantial risk-taking position while working in the trading roles of various banks. We transitioned into managing money in leading hedge fund companies.

He has gone on to greater heights recently, setting up Modular Asset Management, one of Singapore's biggest organic hedge funds, with over $1 billion in assets under management.

Jimmy and I have another thing in common besides our career paths: we were both raised by single parents and are recognised for our grit to succeed. We also share a lot of wine analyses and cooking tips, another avenue where we can compete and strive for perfection.

I must have said something about one of us running a billion-dollar hedge fund one day, right? Congratulations for achieving it! Why did you name it Modular?

Jimmy: The gist of it was that the name captured how I want it to be structured. As a firm, we are already a specialist with the majority of our risk in Asia, which is what we are good at. Coupled with my belief that specialisation beats generalisation, we only hire people who are experts in their own country or product.

Portfolio managers run individual operations called modules, where they focus exclusively on their area of expertise. This also allows the individual modules to grow at their own pace, reflecting the way that different capital markets in Asia are at different stages of development. And this approach means people take responsibility for their own growth and are self-driven.

What was the thought process of scaling up from BlueCrest and JP Morgan Chief Investment Office, strategies from being a PM yourself to owning a business? What challenges did you overcome?

Jimmy: I've always had the belief that in order to succeed, you need to surround yourself with people who are better than you, who are stronger and able to grow even further and larger than you.

Now, how do we make this happen? I view my role here as more of an enabler. There are pros and cons, and the advantage is that if these people grow better and larger than me, I grow together with them. You have to take a long-term view of this. I was always able to return seven to eight per cent with a Sharpe ratio of two to three, yet my focus now is on coaching other people to do that. For me, coaching that skill is harder than actually doing it. Every time I hand over something to someone else – like my China portfolio in 2019 – I feel like I am giving away a part of myself, as well as giving up some of my "personal returns". But it makes perfect sense for the long-term future of the firm, which has to go beyond me.

Have you ever been disappointed in someone you gave your portfolio off to?
Jimmy: From 2017 till now, as I built the fund, I was certainly disappointed sometimes. It was within my expectation range, with a 15 to 20 per cent failure rate. What I didn't expect was that these failures took up a disproportionate amount of my time – one third to half! It always takes longer to solve problems than you think.

Sometimes you have to recognise when failures can't be resolved, and manage your team as they deal with it. Unfortunately, dealing with humans is very different from trading! It is easier to give up a trade position than to give up on a person.

It can also be disappointing when people don't fail outright, but don't meet our expectations either. What **do** you do with a situation like this? That's been a struggle and I have not been able to figure it out.

That's actually even worse – death by a thousand cuts. Sometimes you'd rather it be fast.

We weren't dealt the best cards in life, and had to deal with all sorts of problems in childhood. Can you share some of your darkest moments, and how you recovered from them?

Jimmy: As we've said to each other, we're connected in a way – we're both successful traders and thrived in a dog-eat-dog environment from a young age. A lot of it probably has a lot to do with our background, because there was no safety net. If you didn't win, you could only lose.

We were both raised by single mums. My dad left us with a lot of debt from loansharks, and their runners would lock us in with chains or try to set our home on fire. We knew we couldn't live there any longer, so my brother, my mother and I all lived in different places. We stayed with relatives, but we needed our own place – it was that or be treated like a second-class person.

We got through that, but Mum was rarely home as she had to work several jobs. We lived together again when I was 14, but we were rebellious and turned to crime. My brother didn't complete primary school and by the time I was 14, I had been to the police station seven times for shoplifting, extortion and rioting.

It was too much for Mum, and that year she tried to take her own life but failed. When we called the ambulance to bring her to the hospital, her siblings came by to see her off. "Such a stupid woman. She should have died," one of them muttered.

That was the moment when I realised I didn't need the people who called themselves my family. If they were willing to kick us when we were down, there was nothing they could offer us. Emotionally, I think that was the most challenging part of my upbringing.

It's made us more result-oriented, hasn't it? Can kids with less troubles pick up similar traits?
Jimmy: We're giving so much to our children which we didn't have growing up, but are we handicapping them in the process? No one should go through what we did, yet we must admit it's built resilience in us. I constantly struggle with this.

We can't make them go through the same situations, but we can impart what we've learnt. Resilience can be built in many ways, as long as we understand that we must not fear failure, but use it to become stronger.

Your academic results and resume only open certain doors. A person's character is far more important, and it is family and parenting that build our character. School can teach us knowledge, but that doesn't mean it is all you will ever need.

That's why I believe in giving children the most love we can, while still helping them grow. I don't want my children to work their whole childhoods – after all, an hour spent with you is better than 100 hours spent in even a great school, because they'll look at you and say, "*This* is what a father should be."

Your company is a trailblazer in nurturing future talent as we've seen in the papers. How did your internship programme for students come about?
Jimmy: There were two angles to it. One came by chance – as after all, many times it's better to be lucky than smart. One of our PMs was from a school that sent students to different companies for working experience, but asset management was not included. They approached her and she asked if I could help.

By then we had an established internship programme to find raw talent, from which we had hired many of our team. (We also had a conversion track for experienced team members.) I wanted to see more talent, especially women, and we got a programme running for them. Competition for the few slots available was fierce, the students had to pass a stringent process, including a video interview.

Their school was far stricter about the selection process than we were. We intentionally picked someone who didn't have the best resume, and she did amazingly well! Traders aren't always known for getting along with others, but she had great soft skills and was able to hold her own with colleagues twenty years her senior. I was most impressed.

You've a high-flying career now, and that needs a lot of self-drive and a thirst to become the best. What's your advice to people in school, who want to improve their situation? What three things can they do?

Jimmy: First, have a goal. Even a vague goal is better than none at all, for example, I just want to make my family life a bit better, or an upgrade from a one-room to a three-room flat.

Next, give yourself a timeline. Do you aim to hit your target in five years? Three? Finally, plan the steps needed. To this day, I plan my life five years in advance and take the steps to reach my target. If you don't hit your milestones, it's a sign you need to work harder or adjust your goal.

The process is the most important thing. It's what you do daily to turn aspirations into reality.

You used to get aggressive after a lot of drinks. That's changed, hasn't it?
Jimmy: Absolutely. Until I was 30, I was hard-charging and driven to do more than others. The stress and need to control my emotions led to me internalising much of the anger and frustration I felt.

What changed was the toll it took on my family. I didn't realise it was extending to them, and I found myself getting angry with my wife, my mother and other loved ones. It was an enormous red light.

In 2008, I was attending the very first Singapore Formula One Grand Prix. I drank heavily and caused some damage, breaking many things in the venue and a bone in my hand. I had to go to hospital for emergency surgery ... and that ruined my wife's birthday celebration the next day. Even worse, we had friends in town, and we had embarrassed ourselves in front of them.

That woke me up, and I resolved to learn how to control my emotions and vent my stress, which is why I cook and exercise avidly. I still often look back on that incident.

Many of us actually know what our deepest problems are. But sometimes, it takes a trigger for us to recognise and work on them.

Thank you for sharing this. I'm sure it will inspire lots of people to do better. So how important is a random helping hand? You must have come across many mentors and people who have pointed you the right way over the years. How important is it that you value your roots, and repay them?

Jimmy: That's a tough one! I've never actually met any mentor figures. As much as I wish I'd met someone who had helped me and shaped my career and life, that never happened.

Instead, I've found it best to make things happen, whether such a person shows up or not. I intentionally shaped my studying and my internship so that I could become a trader. Then I tried trading the best products, but people gave me more blockage than help. I had to take risks to get what I wanted.

One person does stand out as an inspiring example of drive and determination: Nicolas, the CIO of an endowment fund. Anyone reading this in our field will know who I'm talking about. By the time I met him eight years ago, he'd already lost half of his tongue to cancer. Yet, he trained himself to speak once more and threw himself into his work, investing everywhere in the world and travelling every week! He loved to eat, drink wine and lived life to the fullest despite adversity.

Six years after I'd gotten to know him, he suffered a recurrence of the cancer and another quarter of his tongue had to be removed. If it recurs again, he will lose it completely, but he doesn't let that slow him down – he has relearned to talk, eat and drink, all the while growing his business.

Now that's an inspiration. There'll always be people who start off worse and end up better than you. But if I had to pick just one source of inspiration, it'd be him.

If I may paraphrase – you always have to find a way, whether you're guided into one or you must make your own.
Jimmy: Indeed. My path was partially blocked in my early career. I wanted to trade Non-Deliverable Forwards, and it was

given to someone else. I took a risk and joined Merrill Lynch, knowing that I would get into trading desks no one wanted, then another risk at Lehman by trading G10 forwards, a new product to me. But that made me different, and those gambles paid off. Then I applied to join JP Morgan Chief Investment Office, which I knew was a gap I needed to fill in order to become a PM at a hedge fund. It was all planned.

You kind of pre-empted my next question. What do you advise people to do differently from the norm, like living overseas?
Jimmy: We've both embraced overseas working experience in the very early part of our careers. It's one of the best things we've ever done.

That's invaluable, because you gain a completely different experience. You are exposed to completely different products, and how other people work. That helps us work alongside members of any culture, so while you still can, take as many opportunities as possible to live and work in other countries. It's harder with the COVID-19 pandemic, but the world will reopen and the chances will come back.

Can you share the principles of how to become a successful investor?
Jimmy: One key principle is that if you know how to take care of your downside, your upside will take care of itself.

On top of that, do what you know. Specialise in what you are good at and be willing to learn something new, though don't expect to learn something for a few days and start trading it! One very strong trader in BlueCrest told me he spent three years studying one market before he dared to put five per cent risk into it. Only after seven years did he feel comfortable having all his risk in that market.

Similarly, I have a module that runs on alternative, unconventional data, for the last three years. That only accounts for five per cent of my risk, but I expect this to grow as we are about hit the inflection point.

How did you put emotions aside and keep going with your work and life, such as after your dog Sparky died?
Jimmy: We were like father and son. He was always there for me, whatever my state, so I've long felt he was the only one who truly listened to me. I knew about a year in advance that he could pass at any time, so with medication (lots of medication) he could still eat, walk and play. I used that year to prepare for the time when we said goodbye.

I asked this question because Paul Tudor Jones told me that life events like these make or break people. They cause traders to suddenly change their style, because they just can't accept the change but they think they can. It's certainly important to know how to let it go, isn't it?
Jimmy: I was lucky that I had a year to mentally prepare. It helped me process it so it wouldn't materially affect the rest of my life.

That said, I was still in denial the day he finally died. "I can still feel his pulse!" I insisted. "He'll wake up tomorrow." But the next morning, his body was so stiff that it was obvious he had left us. My soul was torn in two.

I greatly cut back my social media use, as I realised I had been spending a lot of time posting pictures of him. Over time, it became easier to let go. I don't think I'll be able to completely detach from that loss, though.

Thanks for sharing that! We need to handle our grief well, to accept it rather than fight it or completely ignore it. You can't do nothing with it as well because it's just part of you.

What's Jimmy like without anybody else with him?

Jimmy: I don't like being alone, but neither am I very sociable. I do like to be out with people I like, and if I'm alone I find the time to do things I like to do, like golf or finding my friends and hanging out.

That's how you balance your life. We find the time to do it all, and sometimes we do need some downtime. Sleep it off, because after all, we're more efficient when we're better rested. I used to mistakenly think I was failing if I didn't work until a certain time.

What is the biggest change for you since you first started work? What hasn't changed?

Jimmy: I now have to consider a lot of other people's lives, so I can't decide for myself any longer. How I decide must tie into the well-being of my entire firm, and especially the people that put their faith in me. That's a serious responsibility.

What has not changed, and I know will never change, is that I want to constantly do better for my company and team. Initially, you just want to do better for yourself, but once you're established, it becomes doing better for other people, be they your investors or your colleagues.

Finally, how do we make it even better for the even bigger good? For instance, in Modular, we want to push for the growth of the entire asset management industry in Singapore. Why should our country only be known for the Government Investment Corporation or Temasek? Why can't a privately-owned fund drive the industry forward?

We grow from self to others, then to country and cause. We don't change who we are, we just get the capacity to think bigger.

Many early investors in cryptocurrencies have done well, experiencing triple-digit growth. Can you share your view of cryptos and their future?
Jimmy: Like all disruptive technologies or innovation, it's initially uncomfortable for people. But consider the dot-com bubble and the Y2K fears back in 2000, when we were afraid that critical infrastructure would crash and planes would fall out of the sky. Our uncertainty with crypto and the technologies behind it is something like that.

I do know that the blockchain technology that powers it will survive and thrive. The cycle of acceptance has shortened, so instead of 20 years it will probably take five or ten. What form it takes, I don't know, but I do know it's at the stage the Internet was in 2000. It will become an essential part of your life, and that's already happening with central banks building their own versions, and China pioneering its own digital currency.

Of course, there'll be winners and losers. Think of names like Juniper or Netscape, both of which have disappeared.

Looking back on your life, would you have changed anything? What mistakes have you made and why change those?
Jimmy: No. Even if I had a time machine, it still wouldn't mean I can change the end point. I wouldn't wish some of my experiences on anyone, but they did shape me and I wouldn't change a single thing. I got a cut on my head after being thrown by my dad into a wall, and maybe changing that would make me better-looking. But otherwise, nothing.

One key weakness I struggle with and can't correct enough is not acting fast enough. I'm working on it.

Sometimes you need to give it time, right?
Jimmy: Yes, though I'm generally more worried about downside than upside. I know the power of compounding over time, so if I don't take a great opportunity quickly enough, I lose out.

Have you thought about your legacy and what you want to be remembered for?
Jimmy: Right now, it will be very linked to what Modular can become. As I said, why can't it be the best asset management firm in Singapore, or even in Asia? It should be known for serving the entire industry, and developing talent in Singapore, especially bringing more women into it.

We recently signed up to the United Nations Principles for Responsible Investment, which was an important step for

Modular. I believe that sustainability – environmental, social and governance (ESG) issues – must be infused into our thinking, even for macro investors like us.

We must be very careful about how we want to do it. How do we actually make a difference? It's easy to talk about the environment. It's easy to create scorecards. How do you influence people to make the social and governance changes that are needed?

As difficult as it is, we want to be on the forefront in this, shaping the process together.

We're serious about it, which is why our ESG scorecard was co-developed with the National University of Singapore. I'm trying to fuse all this into the investment process, and it will take time but we're resolving the difficulties we face.

There's a lot of talking, but doing is much more than that. Thanks for your time!
Jimmy: Thank you.

CONCLUSION: BOUNCING BACK HIGHER

> Happiness is really just about four things: perceived control, perceived progress, connectedness (number and depth of your relationships), and vision/meaning (being part of something bigger than yourself).
>
> **Tony Hsieh,** *Delivering Happiness*

I wrote most of this book in late 2019 and early 2020, before the longer-term effects of the COVID-19 pandemic had become known. Like my colleagues, I wanted to be as cautious as possible, and identify any long-term trends in the crypto world before I took any risks.

As I conclude this book, 2020 remains a fresh memory. It's been a watershed year in financial history, and is destined to be mentioned in the same breath as the Great Depression of the 1930s, the post-World War II slump, the collapse of the dot-com bubble in 2001 (not helped by the destruction of the World Trade Center in September) and the great housing recession of 2008. Notice that all of these recessions happened at a time of great global change, and this present pandemic certainly qualifies as such a change. Countries around the world closed their borders, shut down non-essential travel and businesses, and mandated social distancing to try to slow the spread of the virus. Entire industries were brutally tested as customer traffic dried up and many businesses did not survive.

A look at the Bitcoin price chart of 2020 shows that it began the year at $7,200, then experienced a slight rise in value over February and early March, followed by a sharp drop to less than $5,000 as global markets were struck down by the coronavirus. But this needs to be seen in the context of *other* financial instruments, which were similarly affected until governments shored up the markets, and the affected businesses, with stimulus funds. Bitcoin prices had actually recovered to pre-pandemic levels as early as May, and continued to rise thereafter. "While Bitcoin price still remains volatile, it is now a function of an array of factors within the mainstream economy, as opposed to being influenced by speculators looking for quick profits through momentum trades," noted John Edwards in *Investopedia*.[1]

Remember that cryptocurrencies are designed to become more valuable in times of uncertainty and government restriction, not less. Bitcoins also became more sought after as the supply of new bitcoins was reduced in the halving of 11 May, when mining new bitcoins only produced 6.25 new bitcoins per new block, down from 12.5.

This, and stimulus spending by the US and other governments, spurred confidence among investors. "The pandemic shutdown, and subsequent government policy, fed into investors' fears about the global economy and accelerated Bitcoin's rise. At close on November 23, Bitcoin was trading for $18,353," said Edwards, in the *Investopedia* article.

By December, each bitcoin was trading at just under $24,000, but it wasn't done – by the first week of January 2021, it was at a new record price of over $41,000. It hadn't just recovered, but had more than *quadrupled* in value. People were growing more confident that it would live up to its promise.

There were ups and downs over the next few days, an indication that its problem of volatility has not yet been fully solved. There is, however, enough demand to keep its price high over 2021 and beyond, and as blockchains become more widespread, we can have confidence that people will more easily identify ways they can be used.

The most valuable companies today are those that will have a world-changing product tomorrow, and who can prepare best for the day after. As we've seen in the interview of Kyber Network's Loi Luu in Chapter 8, DeFi is taking blockchains into the future and while some speculation is still happening, we can have confidence it's more grounded than the ICOs of the past. DeFi is just getting started, whether or not it involves Bitcoin, so the first cryptocurrency's success means you still have reason to watch the space carefully and invest where you see fit, confident that stability will improve. As Bradley Keoun wrote in *Coindesk*:[2]

> For one, it reinforced the reality that while bitcoin was the oldest and biggest cryptocurrency, it was hardly the most interesting. The digital asset industry and market infrastructure had matured to the point that the competition looked genuine;

rival projects were proving capable of fast-paced innovation, disruption and growth.

In other words, the companies behind such lifesaving services like Amazon or Zoom weren't the only ones to strike it big. If you held on to your bitcoins the entire year, you've made an investment that marries the dynamism of new technology with the assurance of gold. You'll have finished it much richer than when you started, with the endorsement of many a bank and investment fund. It's possible future uses of DeFi and their convergence with AI technology will leave Bitcoin behind, but its nature as *l'argent sans frontieres* means it is likely to remain an important value store, as times grow more and more uncertain.[3]

We're just getting started, and I hope this has helped you take your portfolio into the future with renewed optimism and confidence, tempered by the advice of others, a healthy scepticism and your own tolerance for risk.

A Cautionary Tale
On 18 November 2020, firefighters were summoned to a house fire in New London, Connecticut. It's not clear how it started, but when they reached a shed attached to the house, one of them was heard saying a victim was "barricaded" inside. It remains unclear why he was in there, but by the time venture capitalist, customer service pioneer and former Zappos CEO Tony Hsieh could be rescued, he had inhaled a fatal amount of smoke – nine days later, he was dead at the age of 46, taking the mystery of his final months to the grave with him.

One of the stranger puzzles was how he got a fixation on fire. As Kirsten Grind, James Hagerty and Katherine Sayre wrote in *The Wall Street Journal*,[4] he had bought a mansion in Park City, Utah, and the realtor later visited to find Hsieh had set up 1,000 candles in it. They were, Hsieh had cryptically explained, "a symbol of what life was like in a simpler time."

The article continued:

> Mr. Hsieh became fixated on trying to figure out what his body could live without, according to one friend. He starved himself of food, whittling away to under 100 pounds; he tried not to urinate; and he deprived himself of oxygen, turning toward nitrous oxide, which can induce hypoxia, this person said.

The COVID-19 pandemic had apparently kept him from the non-stop busy-ness he needed, and as the world wound down, his mental health worsened, and he found solace in the bottle and recreational drugs. By the time of his death, Hsieh had been planning to seek help at a clinic in Hawaii, but it was too little, too late. The article pointed out that in investing in communities like Park City and attracting like-minded people to live in them, sometimes by promising to double their previous salaries, Hsieh had created a system of yes-men. They were both dependent on him and reluctant to question his decisions.

In August 2020, he received what was a planned week-long visit by another close friend, pop singer Jewel, who performed for a private audience and abruptly left after only one night. Because Hsieh had (according to *Forbes*) sworn off email and text messaging, a letter from her had to be delivered via FedEx. Part of her strong warning read:[5]

> The people you are surrounding yourself with are either ignorant or willing to be complicit in you killing yourself … If the world could see how you are living, they would not see you as a tech visionary, they would see you as a drug addicted man who is a cliché. That's not how you should go down or be known.

Every single person around Hsieh, Jewel wrote, was on his payroll. That very likely contributed to nobody stopping him from carrying out his final, fatal experiment. (It would later emerge that he was working dangerously on lowering the oxygen level in an enclosed space, and had asked friends to check on him every five minutes.)

Much will no doubt be written about his life and choices, especially his emphasis on friendship and happiness at work over money. In the end, all his wealth did not enable him to make better choices or attract great people to him, it made his addictions worse, stripped away any ability others had to help him change for the better, and amplified his personal weaknesses. His incredible charisma and way with people, normally a strength for any company, turned against him in the end.

That's the result of having lots of money. It's merely a resource, and resources don't make one a better person, just a more influential one. After all, a million dollars in the hands of an entrepreneur is simply going to improve his business; a million dollars in a government official's hands is going to be sliced up according to the priorities he or she must address; and a million dollars in the hands of a crime boss is going to expand criminal activities. Money in itself is just a means of getting things done, what those things are depends on the person holding the money.

It's a sobering thought to close with, but I want to end this book of encouragement with a note to look within ourselves, and find the right people to make up for our weaknesses. It's much more personal and reflective than my previous work, and that's because the worlds of traditional banking and cryptocurrencies alike have taken one beating after another. The year 2020 has been compared to an entire decade's worth of disasters compressed into just one year.

But take heart. As we've seen, fortunes are still being won and lost, and the stock market and other financial institutions have largely been spared the collapses of a decade before. As long as investors keep to the fundamentals of good trading, there will still be a market in good order for many years to come. While COVID-19 has rocked many businesses and cut off revenue to the point where many may never recover, there are also opportunities to rally the economy, and help individual owners in a far more direct way than before.

Perhaps this is the most important lesson we can take away – we need other people, and they need us. It is those companies that will make life better for more people that will succeed in the coming global shift, as the march of technology has proven over and over again.

That's the truth at the heart of capitalism and the free market that I have the privilege to explore every day, and the power it has to lift people out of poverty is needed today more than ever. I'll close with the inspiring words of the late economist Walter E Williams:

> Prior to capitalism, the way people amassed great wealth was by looting, plundering and enslaving their fellow man. Capitalism made it possible to become wealthy by serving your fellow man.

To your success, and all the best as you pay it forward!

Endnotes

1 John Edwards, "Bitcoin's Price History", *Investopedia*, 3 February 2021, at https://www.investopedia.com/articles/forex/121815/bitcoins-price-history.asp.

2 Bradley Keoun, "Bitcoin Prices in 2020: Here's What Happened", *Coindesk*, 31 December 2020, at https://www.coindesk.com/bitcoin-prices-in-2020-heres-what-happened.

3 As explained in my earlier book, *l'argent sans frontières* is French for "money without borders", a play on the medical organisation Médecins Sans Frontières ("Doctors Without Borders").

4 Kirsten Grind, James R Hagerty and Katherine Sayre, "The Death of Zappos's Tony Hsieh: A Spiral of Alcohol, Drugs and Extreme Behavior", *The Wall Street Journal*, 6 December 2020, at https://www.wsj.com/articles/the-death-of-zappos-tony-hsieh-a-spiral-of-alcohol-drugs-and-extreme-behavior-11607264719.

5 Angel Au-Yeung and David Jeans, "Tony Hsieh's American Tragedy: The Self-Destructive Last Months Of The Zappos Visionary", *Forbes*, 4 December 2020, at https://www.forbes.com/sites/angelauyeung/2020/12/04/tony-hsiehs-american-tragedy-the-self-destructive-last-months-of-the-zappos-visionary.

GLOSSARY

This is a glossary of cryptocurrency terms that have come into use since the introduction of Bitcoin in 2009, as well as some financial trading and computing jargon you need to know to understand how it gets its value.

As with the rest of this book, by the time you read this, the information here may not include some of the latest developments. Nevertheless, it's a great base on which to build your understanding of crypto, and barring a similarly huge technological leap, the basic concepts are unlikely to change anytime soon.

And if that leap does happen, don't worry, we'll be on it – and ready to share it – faster than you can make your next trade.

Without further ado, here's the vocabulary you'll need to sound like a crypto pro and know what you're talking about. Words in **bold** type are listed elsewhere in this Glossary.

51 per cent attack
A tampering with the **blockchain** of a **cryptocurrency**, in which the attacking party takes control of more than half the total **mining** power dedicated to adding a new block of data. Such a party will always have the right to add new blocks, and can prevent needed transactions and issue fraudulent, **double-spent**

ones. The risk of a successful attack on a major **token** is minimal, but less popular blockchains may be vulnerable.

Address (cryptocurrency)
An alphanumeric string of characters that makes up your unique **cryptocurrency** ID – the credential that allows you access to the cryptocurrency holdings in your name. **Blockchains** are the publicly accessible records of transactions from one address to another.

The same user can have multiple addresses, in the same way they can use different email addresses depending on the need.

Altcoin
Short for "alternative coin", or any **crypto** other than **Bitcoin**. Examples include **Ether**, LiteCoin, Ripple, Dash and (at this writing) thousands more.

ASIC
Application-Specific Integrated Circuit, a device similar to CPUs and graphics cards. These use their processing power solely for mining and decrypting crypto in a **mining rig**.

Bitcoin (BTC)
The first **cryptocurrency**, introduced in 2009 by Satoshi Nakamoto and a small community of pioneers. It is the standard against which all others are measured; you'll generally see a list of attributes such as value, transaction speed, privacy and others that say how the **crypto** differs from Bitcoin itself.

For this book, capitalised "Bitcoin" refers to the currency proper, while lowercase "bitcoin(s)" refers to specific amounts of it. Today a single bitcoin is worth thousands of dollars, and trading of smaller amounts such as milli-bitcoins, micro-bitcoins or **satoshis** is more commonplace.

To resolve the limitations of Bitcoin as designed, hard **forks** in mid-2016 and late 2017 produced branching cryptocurrencies Bitcoin Cash (BCH) and Bitcoin Gold (BCG).

Block

A new entry to a **blockchain** ledger, consisting of sending and receiving IDs, and the amount involved. New blocks are **mined** into circulation, with their payout (in the case of **Bitcoin**) halving every four years.

Blockchain

An encrypted, almost incorruptible ledger of transactions from one address to another that is attached to your user account, updated several times hourly; six times, in the case of **Bitcoin**.

This is the official record of what and how much (of potentially anything, not just **crypto**) you own, receive, sell or give away.

Coin

See "**cryptocurrency**".

Composability

The ability of different parts of a software program, or different programs entirely, to seamlessly work together to produce a result that was not possible before.

Crypto
Short for "**cryptocurrency**". It refers to the fact that cryptocurrencies begin as encrypted "blocks" of data that must be decoded through **mining** – usually through application of vast amounts of computing power.

Cryptocurrency
A financial product (with a stock-like variable monetary value) consisting of recorded, permanent agreements between computers and user identities, with new units made available by **cryptography**-breaking **mining**. These are decentralised with records updated by everyone in the product's network, rather than controlled by a central bank. Attractive due to its **pseudonymity** and theoretical immunity to interference from governments.

Specific cryptocurrencies have come to be known as simply "**coins**" or "**tokens**".

Cryptography
The science of secure, tamper-proof communication through encoding information in an unintelligible form, using a mathematical operation; to be decoded by the recipient's computer using a key sent to it, or by brute-force guessing billions of solutions a second. The latter is the approach behind **crypto mining**.

DAO
Decentralised Autonomous Organisation, that is, a group of **Ethereum** smart contracts written to serve a specific purpose.

Dark Web
The part of the Internet where hidden message boards, drug sales and other illegal activity flourish, accessible only through specially-built Web browsers designed not to leave an electronic "trail" of their user history. Needless to say, it's popular with criminals and law enforcement agents.

Crypto is popular here due to its pseudonymous nature, but remember it's simply a tool, it's only as good or evil as the person using it. Not to be confused with "**Deep Web**".

Decentralisation
The distribution of authority and decision-making power throughout an entire organisation, creating autonomous units that work independently towards a common goal. In the context of **cryptocurrencies**, this means users form a **P2P** network with no single point where it can be shut down.

Deep Web
The parts of the Internet that are accessible only to users with valid credentials, such as a user ID and password. Most Internet utilities such as online shopping accounts, email and many more are technically part of the Deep Web. Not to be confused with "**Dark Web**".

Derivative
A financial instrument in the form of a contract regarding an underlying store of value, like a cryptocurrency or stock. These "derived" products include forwards, futures, options, swaps and

more, and are usually bought and sold at exchanges, without the underlying entity having to trade.

Double spending
The error of digital money being "paid" to a recipient, while the sender can simply copy it and keep the money they have supposedly "sent". The result is that the same sum of money can be spent over and over again, a problem blockchains were built to solve.

A **cryptocurrency** can be compromised and double spending set up in the event of a successful **51 per cent attack**.

ETF
Exchange-Traded Fund, a fund that is traded like an ordinary stock but actually combines various shares chosen by its managers. It is widely believed that **cryptocurrencies** may eventually be traded this way.

Ether (ETH)
The traded cryptocurrency used to raise funds for, and run, new projects on **Ethereum**.

Ethereum
A blockchain environment envisioned as a "world computer", where blockchain-based applications can be created and run, and transactions made through pre-programmed "**smart contracts**". Projects are funded using the **cryptocurrency** known as **ether**, and allocated space using a resource known as **gas**.

GLOSSARY

Exchange (cryptocurrency)
Similar to a stock exchange, a central online hub where **crypto** prices are tracked and you can order or sell specific quantities with **fiat**. Like with stock markets, some exchanges are more reliable than others.

Fiat
Traditional money, such as US dollars, euros and other currencies. The term is used in the context of payment for amounts of **cryptocurrency**, and it is so-called because it is approved by government authority.

Fork
An operation that splits a **blockchain** into two separate ones, usually for technical reasons such as the block size limit in **Bitcoin**. Forks can be "soft" or "hard" in **crypto**: a soft fork retains compatibility with the existing **blockchain**, while a hard fork creates an entirely new **cryptocurrency** with no link to the old one.

Futures
Derivative contracts where an asset is set up to be bought or sold at a later date, at an agreed price rather than the price when the sale happens. This manages risk by "locking in" the price of a good, although the buyer and seller assume some risk of losing money.

Gas
A special unit used by **Ethereum** to measure the "work" needed to perform a particular action, to ensure that the right amount of **ether** is paid to perform it.

Hash
A mathematics-based cypher used to encrypt data and ensure it is securely transmitted. New **crypto** units are released in a hashed form, and the act of providing computing power to break the hashes is known as **mining**.

Hash rate
A measure of a **mining rig**'s computing power, based on how many guesses at solving the **hash** it can make per second. A higher hash rate means faster guessing, and a higher chance of winning the race for the right to add to the **blockchain**.

Initial Coin Offering (ICO)
The initial sale of a percentage of custom-made **crypto** by a startup to investors, usually for public fundraising; the investors stand to gain if the new crypto is successful and rises in value. This is similar to a new company's first sale of its stocks or an Initial Public Offering (IPO).

Due to the fact that ICOs are open to the entire community, many startups opt for them rather than the more traditional model of venture capital.

Initial Exchange Offering (IEO)
The sale of **crypto** issued by a new startup through a crypto **exchange**, instead of directly to customers. This is to increase assurance that the money will be used fairly and the project is not a scam.

Lightning Network
A **cryptocurrency** transfer protocol that aims to make transactions instant, solving the delay in verifying them through miners.

Mining
The act of transacting by adding your computing power to efforts to decrypt "blocks" of **crypto** as they are released. The computers that decrypt each hash are called mining rigs, and their owners ("miners") are rewarded if they are the first to complete the decryption.

Mining farm
A purpose built facility where hundreds or thousands of linked computers are set up for **mining** crypto as quickly as possible, through combining their calculating power into a single, powerful **mining rig**.

More power means a higher chance of being the first to break the **hash**, and earning the resulting payout. They profit by having their share of the mining proceeds exceed their prodigious operating costs, especially in the form of power bills, maintenance and cooling.

Access to a farm's processing power is often sold on the Internet, with the promise of a share of the proceeds.

Mining rig
A computer running **cryptocurrency-mining** software.

Mint
A term by **Nakamoto** for a bank or other financial authority that verifies transactions to be error-free. Not to be confused with government mints that create physical notes and coins.

Nakamoto, Satoshi
Pseudonym used by the as yet unknown inventor(s) of **Bitcoin**, **blockchain** and **cryptocurrency** as a concept. Several people and groups have been suspected of being Nakamoto, but no conclusive evidence has been found.

Open source
A license arrangement that makes software and the underlying source code freely available for anyone to use, modify and re-distribute as they see fit, without paying or needing permission from the original creators. This allows public users all over the world to study, adapt and collaborate on projects.

Bitcoin and **Ethereum** are examples of open-source **cryptos**, and there are also programs like OpenOffice, a free alternative to Microsoft's Office suite of programs.

Options
Derivative contracts to obtain the right (not the obligation) to buy an underlying asset at the value it had on the date the option is bought, by a specific time in the future. This hedges against the asset's loss in value, and produces a profit should the asset's value rise.

Peer-to-peer (P2P)
A decentralised network of computers where every member can both request and carry out a service; the opposite of a client-provider model.

Pseudonymity
The property of online identities like **crypto addresses**, email or Facebook accounts; they do not have to be in your real name should you so choose not to use it. Some identifying information is still present, such as in **blockchain**, for example, the transaction history of your **Bitcoin address**.

Not to be confused with anonymity, which refers to a complete lack of identifying information.

Satoshi
Slang for the smallest tradeable unit of **Bitcoin**, named in honour of its creator. One **satoshi** is equivalent to one hundred millionth ($1/10^8$) of a bitcoin.

Smart contract
An automated, pre-arranged series of transactions in **Ethereum** that is set to trigger when certain conditions are met. For example, a smart contract can be made to pay out amounts of **ether** to various parties when a purchase is confirmed.

Security Token Offering (STO)
A sale of a startup's security **tokens**, which function in the same way as shares and are subject to the same regulations, and are only available to accredited investors.

Stablecoin
A **crypto** with backing from various other sources, such as fiat money. For instance, Facebook's Diem is backed by the values of the US dollar.

Token
See "**cryptocurrency**".

Wallet
Your secure user identity linked to your **address**, which determines your access to your own **bitcoins**. A hardware wallet might be used, in which a physical device connects to your computer via USB and authenticates your identity as well.

Wiki
A shared article board that anyone in the community can edit. The word comes from Wikipedia, and is Hawaiian for "quick".

APPENDIX

I have included this article by Brent Donnelly (on the next page) as it is a lifesaver and it is appropriate for a book like *Deflated* to host it. It applies to all new hedge fund managers and the Robinhood traders of the world that are diving into financial markets trading. Most of us do not see a second chance and it is great to learn from the mistakes that Brent and I have made.

> "Of course there is always a reason for fluctuations, but the tape does not concern itself with the why and wherefore. It doesn't go into explanations. I didn't ask the tape why when I was fourteen, and I don't ask it today, at forty. The reason for what a certain stock does today may not be known for two or three days, or weeks, or months. But what the dickens does that matter? Your business with the tape is now not tomorrow. The reason can wait. But you must act instantly or be left."
>
> —Edwin Lefèvre
> **author of *Reminiscences of a Stock Operator***

DAY ONE ADVICE FOR NEW HEDGE FUND PORTFOLIO MANAGERS

Over the first six months of 2021, there was a mass influx of new hedge fund PMs. Many of these traders left bank trading seats to explore potentially greener pastures. I have occupied both seats, and so here I offer some advice to new hedge fund PMs. I present this advice with the utmost humility; I have had plenty of good years and plenty of disappointing ones.

Here goes:

1) Understand the metagame
Your contract probably has a stop loss in it, but you should also be 100% certain what your real stop loss is. The two numbers are probably not the same! Also, what kind of intraday, daily and weekly volatility will your boss find mildly, or very disturbing? There are the printed rules of the game and then the actual rules. Make sure you know both. Stay away from management pain points.

Your first goal is to prove yourself as a good risk manager. Self-policing is important. Nobody wants a phone call from management, ever ... but especially not in Year One.

2) Start slow
You want to show the firm what a good hire you are by putting up a 3% return in Month One. If anything, though, that will probably set off alarm bells for high volatility, not elicit high fives for stellar returns. If you are going to succeed at a hedge

fund, that success will be measured in years, not months. Play the long game and get settled before you get aggressive. There is substantial path dependence in a hedge fund seat.

Sprinting out of the gates is a bad strategy!

No matter how strong your view when you sit down on Day One, there is too much path dependence. You cannot be max aggressive. Even if you are placing what you think is an 80/20 bet, if the 20% comes up, you are hobbled, your confidence is impaired and that can threaten your liftoff. It's not worth the risk.

Start slow, build the base and be like a call option with limited downside and unlimited upside. You cannot have the same risk appetite on Day One with zero P&L in the coffers as you can have on Day 274 when you are up 15 million dollars. In an ideal world, you should always vary your risk appetite based on conviction and market opportunity. But in the real world, you need to start slow and build risk over time.

Also, there is something special and scary about the zero bound in P&L. Let's say a hypothetical trader named Steven Kirk wants to make $10 million this year and his stop loss is $4 million. He will find that going from +$2 million to +$1 million feels significantly less bad than going from +$500k to -$500k, even though both are P&L declines of $1 million. Any red number next to your name feels bad. This is consistent with loss aversion theory which tells us that if a gain gives us x pleasure, a loss of the same magnitude gives us 2x pain.

This is not all just psychological, though. As Steve's P&L falls below zero, his ability to take risk (his leverage) decreases. There is a non-linear real-world impact of losses as he moves below zero and closer to his stop loss. When you are below zero P&L, you wear a slowly-tightening straitjacket.

Remember: even if your stop loss is $4 million, you are in big trouble trading-wise way before then, because you will need to reduce your position size in order to avoid getting the shoulder tap. Also, if you start with a big loss, you run into the Problem of Percentages. As you probably know, if you lose 1%, you need to make more than 1% to get back to flat. That's annoying. Here is a chart for your enjoyment:

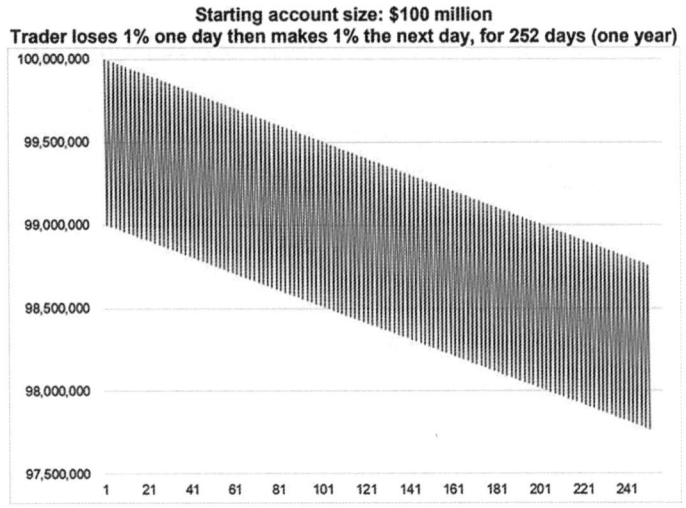

This volatility drag is painful and important.

The goal is to get safely away from the zero bound and then when a mega-opportunity arrives and you have a cushion ... go for it. If Steve is +$1.5 million on February 25 and there is a fantastic opportunity, he is in a position to risk a bigger chunk of cash on the idea without worrying about sinking underwater.

3) Play your own game

Nobody is watching you as intensely as you are watching yourself. Don't avoid a trade because it "seems dumb" or is too micro, etc. Your job is to make money and generally the only thing your boss cares about is your vol and your P&L. Do you want to be smart, or make money?

4) Avoid style drift

If you have been a spot FX trader your whole life, and you go to a hedge fund, your brain is going to be like: "Whoa look at all these flashing numbers, this looks fun!" Kid in candy store. Don't start piling into a short wheat position just because you can. Of the people I have seen rapidly and unceremoniously booted from hedge funds, style drift was often a big part of the story. They hired you because you have an edge in your product(s). Yes, there is a lot to learn by touring other assets and markets, but make sure you spend most of your time focused on markets where you are expert.

5) Be careful when they increase your capital

When you perform well, you will probably get an increase in capital. Remember that you are trading and getting paid in dollars, not basis points. If you make 10% on your initial allocation of $100 million, then they up you to $200 million and you lose 5%, you're back to flat. That's not good! If your allocation doubles, don't just double all your position sizes right away. Scale into your new capital.

Also keep in mind that the moment your capital increases is the moment you are most likely to be overconfident. A) You have been crushing it, otherwise the increase would not have happened in the first place and B) the increase itself is strong validation for your ego. Don't be overconfident! In fact, the day you get an increase in capital, you should turtle a bit and get defensive until the overconfidence risk passes. Time is the best cure for every extreme emotion.

6) Identify where the world is in the macro cycle

Are you joining as a commodity PM in 2012? As an FX carry trader in 2006? As an oil trader in 2016? The fact that you have been hired to the role you were hired for might have information content. Also, unless you are a very short term trader, the stage of the cycle should impact your trading bias. In early 2009, after the Fed, Treasury, Europe and China changed all the rules, one famous investor put a Post-It note on his monitor that read "Long or flat". Depending on what product you trade, a similar Post-It might be appropriate.

7) Find other ways to add value

Sure a PM's main value is the P&L, but people that add value in other ways have more runway. Be an information hub, volunteer to meet investors, overcommunicate with your risk manager, walk around the floor and get to know people. If you are more than just a number, your implicit stop loss is wider and you have a greater probability of success. Furthermore, there is information in talking to people. If 19 out of 20 PMs at your firm are bearish stonks, it's time to add to your longs.

8) Relax and have fun

It's hard to have perspective when you sit down at a hedge fund for the first time. On the one hand, the stakes seem higher than ever. That is scary. On the other hand... You made it! You're living the dream. Look around and see how far you have come. You are probably there for a reason.

Believe in yourself, relax and get to work.

***

Brent Donnelly is President of Spectra Markets. He has been trading professionally since 1995 and is the author of *Alpha Trader* (2021) and *The Art of Currency Trading* (Wiley, 2019). He writes a widely-read, highly-respected macro and FX daily called AM/FX. Over the course of his career, he has been a market maker, trader and senior manager at some of the top banks in foreign exchange.

Brent has extensive experience trading currencies, FX options, stock index futures, NASDAQ stocks and commodities. He is a respected macro thinker with the unique perspective of a senior risk taker. He has been quoted by, or featured in, the *Economist*, *Epsilon Theory*, *Real Vision*, *The Wall Street Journal*, *Financial Times*, *Bloomberg* and CNBC.

Brent has been a senior FX trader at HSBC, head of G10 Spot FX Trading at Citi New York and Managing Director and Head of FX Trading at Nomura New York. He was also a portfolio manager at a major hedge fund in Connecticut for three years

You can contact Brent at brentdonnelly@att.net and on Twitter at @donnelly_brent.

ACKNOWLEDGEMENTS

Thank you my dearest mom, FLY, for risking her whole life with one trade – me. That trade was funded with the help of my granny; the late Uncle Steve; the kindest Uncle Wai and the warmest Auntie Lai Yee.

I would like to especially thank my lovely wife, Hsin, for tirelessly guiding me in the right direction of life. You are the most selfless person in this world.

Xiao, Han and Jue, my three little ones, have been super supportive – yes, some of these wallets will go to you soon.

My bosses and mentors – I am nothing without you: Mark Johnson, Khoo Seow Chiong, CK Lam, David Hong, David Dredge, Driss Ben Brahim, Guy Saidenberg, David Chan, Paul Jones, Neh Thaker, Roberto Hoornweg and Tony Hall.

Thank you, Master Vin, for always shining a leading light.

Stepping into the NUS Computer Science glass building in 2016 changed my life; I owe it to the profs and student friends I met there. Specially Beng Chin and Gene Yan, thanks for the guidance.

Last but not least, my crypto comrades in Kyber Network and Digix Global. Thanks for allowing me to participate in these glorious projects..

ABOUT THE AUTHOR

Leng Hoe Lon leads a set of diverse macro traders in the ten different local offices in the region for Standard Chartered Bank. He has over two decades of experience in trading and investing in financial markets across Singapore, London and Hong Kong. In 2011, he switched to the buy-side, following his investing dreams, to join Tudor Investment Corporation as a global macro portfolio manager focusing on Asian markets.

At 40 years old, Hoe Lon explored new horizons and dived into the tech world of discoveries and start-ups. He spent substantial time in the National University of Singapore and founded, invested in, and advised start-ups in AI and blockchain. During these two years, he played a seasoned financier to the nascent market and published a book, *Decrypted: A Financial Trader's Take on Cryptocurrency*.

Hoe Lon was brought up in Bukit Bintang, Kuala Lumpur, and graduated with an Accounting Degree from the University of Warwick in the UK. He has been a CFA Chartered Holder since 2001. In having a lucky path in life, Hoe Lon regularly gives back to keep the "luck" going. Hoe Lon happily devotes a lot of his time with his mom, FLY, his beloved wife, Hsin, and his children, Xiao, Han, and Jue.

ABOUT THE CO-AUTHOR

Pearlin Siow runs Boss Of Me, a boutique book-writing agency that specialises in helping people write as well as publish books. Together with her team of content specialists, she has written several bestselling biographies for top entrepreneurs and companies in Singapore. Her clients range from billionaires to stay-at-home mothers. Connect with her at www.bossofme.sg

ABOUT THE COVER ARTIST

Aaron Gan is the 2015 UOB Painting of the Year, Gold Award, Established Artist Category, Singapore winner. Born in Singapore in 1979, Gan graduated with a Bachelor of Commerce (Dean's List) from the University of Western Australia in 2003. In 2012, he gave up his corporate career to become a professional artist.

With his exuberant painting style, Gan has earned many sell-out shows under his belt. He showcases regularly in Singapore and internationally and his works have graced the collections of many corporations and institutions. He has also collaborated with many intenational brands. His website is https://aarongan.com

FUNDRAISING FOR FUTUREMAKERS

Three years ago, Leng Hoe Lon wrote *Decrypted*, a book on cryptocurrency. Through book sales, he raised over USD120,000 for the charity, Seeing is Believing. The funds were used to fight against avoidable blindness in communities that needed them most.

With his second book, *Deflated*, he hopse to fundraise for Futuremakers by Standard Chartered. This is a global initiative to tackle inequality and promote greater economic inclusion.

The unequal impact of COVID-19

In the last three years, the world we know has changed dramatically – no thanks to COVID-19.

Everyone is at risk of infection and we have our own unique battles to fight, but not all of us have suffered equally.

Data from the World Bank show that income losses and hunger are more common among households in poorer countries. Within countries, employment and income losses were felt most acutely by vulnerable workers, women, youth and the less educated.

The risk is equal but the suffering is more acute in some segments of our community. And it is not surprising that the recovery will also be unequal.

Helping our youths build resilience for the future
If our future success depends on our youths today, then we need to do something to help them through this global challenge.

About Futuremakers by Standard Chartered Foundation
Social and economic inequality. The growing income gap within and between countries. These are common global challenges though they are most felt acutely in emerging markets.

By 2030, 1% of the world's population will own two-thirds of its wealth. COVID-19 has made this worse as the vulnerable and disadvantaged youths have been especially impacted.

Standard Chartered believes that social and economic inclusion leads to more prosperous and sustainable communities. Donations to the Standard Chartered Foundation (a registered charity in England and Wales charity number 1184946, company number 11968592) supports Futuremakers by Standard Chartered, the Bank's global initiative to tackle inequality and promote greater economic inclusion for disadvantaged youths in our communities. Futuremakers aims to raise USD75 million by 2023 to help our youths learn, earn and grow.

To date, the Bank has contributed USD57 million to Futuremakers programmes, which also supports COVID-19 economic recovery. Its programmes have impacted more than 477,000 young people across 35 markets.

All funds raised for Futuremakers by Standard Chartered will be matched by Standard Chartered PLC up to a limit of USD5 million per year.